One-of-a-Kind QUILT LABELS

Unique Ideas for a Special Finishing Touch

Thea Nerud

CREDITS

President • *Nancy J. Martin*
CEO • *Daniel J. Martin*
Publisher • *Jane Hamada*
Editorial Director • *Mary V. Green*
Managing Editor • *Tina Cook*
Technical Editor • *Jane Townswick*
Design Director • *Stan Green*
Illustrator • *Robin Strobel*
Cover and Text Designer • *Trina Stahl*
Photographer • *Brent Kane*

That Patchwork Place® is an imprint of Martingale & Company®.

One-of-a-Kind Quilt Labels:
Unique Ideas for a Special Finishing Touch

Martingale & Company
20205 144th Avenue NE
Woodinville, WA 98072-8478 USA
www.martingale-pub.com

Printed in Canada
09 08 07 06 05 04   8 7 6 5 4 3 2 1

Mission Statement

Dedicated to providing quality products and service to inspire creativity.

Library of Congress Cataloging-in-Publication Data
Nerud, Thea.
One-of-a-Kind Quilt Labels / Thea Nerud.
p. cm.
Includes bibliographical references.
ISBN 1-56477-535-6
1. Quilts—Labeling—Design. 2. Labels—Design. I. Title.
TT835.N463 2004
746.46'02'78—dc22

2004010486

DEDICATION

To Dana, Dina, and Norman

ACKNOWLEDGMENTS

It's Dana's fault! Dana Kinder machine quilted many of my quilts. She oohed and aahed over the label for each one and asked me to teach classes at her home business, Wild Rose Quilt House, in Spokane, Washington. After the quilt-label class, she told me I needed to put the information in a book. I ignored this advice until my life partner, Norman Samish, saw the label on a quilt I made for our neighbors' new baby. Then he joined the chorus with, "That needs to go into a book."

Okay! I called my-daughter-the-quilt-goddess, Dina Pappas, to find out how to do that. She referred me to her publisher, Martingale & Company, and the process began. Thanks go to all the people at Martingale, especially Karen Soltys and Terry Martin. The photography of Brent Kane and graphics by Robin Strobel made it possible to show what I meant. My technical editor, Jane Townswick, made the editing process almost painless. I appreciate her consideration and expertise.

As I wrote this book, the students in my classes were a great source of support and guidance. Their questions and comments highlighted areas that needed better coverage. Dawn Fifer, owner of The Briar Patch quilt shop in Spokane, introduced me to Bubble Jet Set 2000, that wonderful stuff that lets me make my own printable fabric. Karen Buck, quilter and author, provided machine-embroidery samples for the book at the last minute.

Thank you one and all for helping me turn my bright ideas into a real book.

Contents

Introduction

When my children were young their clothing always bore little labels that I had ordered from a display in a fabric store, which read "An Original by Thea Nerud." My first quilts featured embroidered messages, such as "Warmest Wishes, with Love, from Mom, 1965." Not a lot of information, but enough to convey my sentiments and document the year in which each quilt was completed. Since then, I've been exposed to the work of many first-class quilters and artists and have learned the importance of documenting a complete provenance for quilts as well as for other artwork and handcrafted items.

Almost every quilter I talk with either owns or knows of a mystery quilt in the family: an unsigned, undocumented quilt. The original owner may have known where it came from and who made it and approximately when, but that knowledge is often lost when the quilt is passed on to the next generation.

I have my own mystery quilt project, which is a set of nine Crazy quilt blocks given to me by my mother-in-law. She thought the blocks had been pieced by one of her great aunts, but I may never know the name of the quilter or when the blocks were made. The only clue is a ribbon on one block commemorating the "Fourth Reunion of the 2nd Iowa Cavalry, 1889." The name of the ancestor who fought in the Civil War may never be known, but I continue to search for this information because the blocks will be passed down through my family.

Thus began my mission to get *all* quilts signed and labeled. Documentation can be added to quilts both new and old. Even a label like "Bought at Goodwill in Spokane, WA, 1988 by Thea Nerud" is better than nothing.

I've tried just about every possible method of labeling quilts. My first attempts featured simple, embroidered lettering. Cross-stitching also made pretty labels, but even minimal information took up a lot of space. Drawing with ink on fabric wasn't entirely satisfactory either. Even though I had taken a college course in calligraphy, my hand-lettered labels made with fabric pens looked inept, if not downright dorky. Later, I began to quilt information into the background or borders of a quilt, including the name of the quilt, my name, and the completion date.

In the early 1990s I began experimenting with computer-printed labels. I taped fabric to stiff paper and then ran it through my printer. It usually took two or three tries to yield a successful printing, and the ink washed out unless I coated it with anti-fray fluid. Messy! The anti-fray fluid also made the printed letters blur and dim.

When iron-on transfer films became available I thought they were wonderful, and now you can even make or buy colorfast fabric to use with an ink-jet printer. More and better products continue to appear almost daily. I'm waiting for an absolutely waterproof and colorfast ink-jet ink that will print on untreated fabric. Until then, the products discussed in this book come closest to my ideal labeling media.

I began teaching computer quilt-label classes in 2002, and that class material is included in this book. By showing a fast and easy way to make beautiful, legible quilt labels, I hope to encourage and facilitate the labeling of all quilts. When you see how easy it is to make labels, I hope you'll join me in expanding on the basic label to play with settings and decorate your label creations. I would love to see pictures of your labels as you go on to make your own special projects. You may email photos to me at yourlabels@theaquilts.com.

Thea Nerud

Why Label Your Quilts?

One reason for documenting a quilt's origins is that we forget things. Quilts often last for generations. Future owners should be able to tell who made a quilt, when it was made, the reason it was made, and where the quiltmaker was from. In addition, consider the following reasons for labeling quilts.

VALUE

A quilt can have significant value, both monetary and emotional. Quilts signed by the quiltmaker are more valuable than unsigned quilts, so take your permanent pen and sign your quilt (in addition to creating a label for it). A label might come loose or be intentionally removed, but a permanent-ink signature will always be part of the quilt. Adding a label that specifies the quiltmaker's and recipient's names, the year in which the quilt was made, and the occasion for which the quilt was made provides more value, on both monetary and emotional levels, than leaving a quilt undocumented.

SECURITY

I am so sorry to have to say this, but quilts occasionally get stolen. A label gives proof of ownership and makes a stolen quilt harder to sell. Identifying a lost or stolen quilt is easier if it carries a detailed label. For the most secure type of label, make it part of the quilt's backing. Either piece the label into the backing or stitch it onto the backing and then cut away the backing fabric behind the label before quilting the quilt. If a label is made part of the quilt back and then quilted over, it is nearly impossible to remove, making the quilt less valuable to thieves.

MEANING

Now to the heart of why people make quilts. Quilts add purpose and meaning and beauty to our lives. They help us express our depth of feeling and our artistic talent. A gift card might get lost, but a quilt label is seen and treasured each time someone handles a quilt. The thought, care, and emotion that go into making a quilt can be expressed on a label and touch hearts for years to come.

What to Include on a Quilt Label

At the absolute minimum, include the name of the quiltmaker and the city, state, and year in which the quilt was made. Also consider including:

- Name of the quilt
- Quilt style or pattern name
- Dimensions
- Name of recipient(s)
- Occasion for making the quilt
- Date of the occasion commemorated or celebrated
- Name of the quilter, if different from the quiltmaker
- Special messages or quotations

For women who have married, include your maiden name as well as your married name on your quilt labels. This identifies you and your family relationships most precisely. Genealogy buffs will applaud you.

Labeling Comparison Chart

Only those materials and tools you might not have on hand are listed. Standard sewing equipment, such as irons and ironing boards, are not included.

Method	Special Materials & Equipment	Plusses	Other Considerations	Care
Hand lettering with permanent ink (pages 9–10)	• Permanent markers • Freezer paper	• Durable • Colorfast • Safe for baby quilts	• Appropriate when a handcrafted look is desired • Moderately space efficient • Requires light- to medium-value fabric	• Washable • Safe to iron
Hand lettering with wax crayons (page 11)	• Wax crayons • Freezer paper	• Durable • A fun way to involve children	• Appropriate when a handcrafted look is desired • Requires a very large labeling area • Requires light fabrics • Requires heat-setting; if care isn't taken, wax could smear on iron	Requires gentle washing, which makes this method inappropriate for baby quilts (which call for frequent washing), unless the quilt will be hung on a wall rather than put to daily use
Hand embroidery (page 12)	• Embroidery needle • Embroidery floss	• Durable • Colorfast • Safe for baby quilts	• Appropriate when a handcrafted look is desired • Requires a large labeling area • Depending on thread color, works with either light or dark fabrics	Care needs depend on type of thread. If cotton threads are used, label will be washable and safe to iron.
Machine embroidery (pages 12–13)	• Sewing machine capable of embroidering text or a dedicated embroidery machine • Thread(s) • Fabric stabilizer	• Durable • Colorfast • Safe for baby quilts	• Requires a large labeling area • Depending on thread color, works with either light or dark fabrics	Care depends on type of thread. Cotton threads (and most polyesters) will be washable and safe to iron.

Method	Special Materials & Equipment	Plusses	Other Considerations	Care
Cross-stitch (pages 15–18)	• Aida cloth or waste canvas • Embroidery needles • Embroidery floss	• Durable • Colorfast • Safe for baby quilts	• Appropriate when a handcrafted look is desired • Requires a large labeling area • Depending on thread color, works with either light or dark fabrics	• Washable • Safe to iron
Commercial printable fabric (pages 22–23)	Computer and ink-jet printer*	• Highly space efficient • Widely available • Anything you can print on paper, you can print on fabric	• Durability unknown • Costs more than $3 per 8½" x 11" sheet • White and cream are the only color options	• Care varies; read product documentation for washing and care instructions. • Wash before attaching to a baby quilt. • To prevent ink from bleeding in pooled liquid, dry on an old towel.
Homemade printable fabric (pages 22–23)	• Computer and ink-jet printer* • 100% cotton or silk fabric • Color fixative (Bubble Jet Set 2000 & Bubble Jet Set Rinse) • Freezer paper	• Highly space efficient • Anything you can print on paper, you can print on fabric	• Durability unknown • Costs less than $1 per 8½" x 11" sheet • More time-consuming than buying ready-made printable fabric • Can use any light- to medium-value fabric	• Washable • Safe to iron • Wash before attaching to a baby quilt. • To prevent ink from bleeding in pooled liquid, dry on an old towel.
Iron-on transfers (pages 20–22)	• Computer and ink-jet printer* • Iron-on transfer • sheets (for dark or light fabric)	• Highly space efficient • Anything you can print on paper, you can print on transfers	• Cost ranges from $1 to $2 per sheet • Colorfastness unknown • Transfers available for light or dark fabric • Stiffens fabric	• Washable • Hot iron will melt transfer (see tips for handling transfers on pages 21 and 22).

*If you don't have access to a computer and an ink-jet printer, try your local quilt shop. Some shops will let you use their ink-jet printers for a fee. You might also try a copy shop, but keep in mind that many of them refuse to run fabric through their machines.

Remedial Labels for Unsigned Quilts

IT IS NEVER too late to label an unsigned or undocumented quilt or other handcrafted treasure. Hand stitching a label to an old or vintage quilt will not damage the quilt, and it will preserve all known and verified information with the quilt itself.

If the information you have about a quilt is sketchy, you can always cite the source of the information. For example, I can note the date on which my mother-in-law gave me nine Crazy quilt blocks and include it on a label that stays with the blocks. If the fabric in a quilt can be dated, that information can be included on the label.

People often know who made their quilts and the name of the person(s) to whom they were given. Remember that the next generation will have no information if you don't provide it now.

If you want to give extensive information, photographs of the quiltmaker and recipient make great additions to a label. Birth, death, and marriage dates, and the way a quilt was handed down through a family, also can be included.

You don't have to limit labels to quilts. Small, computer-printed labels in an 8-point font are unobtrusive when hand sewn to crocheted items, knitted garments, embroidered linens, and other handcrafted items. I use them to label doilies and pillowcases made by my grandma. I also use them for doll clothes, clothing, and small quilts. Rather than try to hem such small labels, I simply cut them out and seal the edges with anti-fray fluid.

DIMENSIONS: ENVELOPE 5½" x 5", CARD 4½" x 8"

A label for an old quilt, telling how it was passed down through the family. On the back of the same label, pictures show the quilter and recipients around the time the quilt was made.

WHAT *NOT* TO DO TO OLD QUILTS

- Do not mar or deface the quilt.
- Do not mark directly on the quilt.
- Do not machine stitch a label onto the quilt.
- Do not use adhesives or fusible products to attach a label to the quilt.
- Do not present as fact information that has not been verified.

Hand Lettering

Experiment with the following techniques for hand lettering and determine which ones you like best.

INKED LETTERING

Permanent, waterproof, and fade-proof fabric pens allow you to hand letter labels and add colorful touches like the stenciled iris shown below. It can be difficult to write directly on fabric, so iron freezer paper to the wrong side of the label to keep the fabric from shifting as you write. To keep the lettering straight, use a ruler to mark guidelines on the freezer paper before you press it to the fabric.

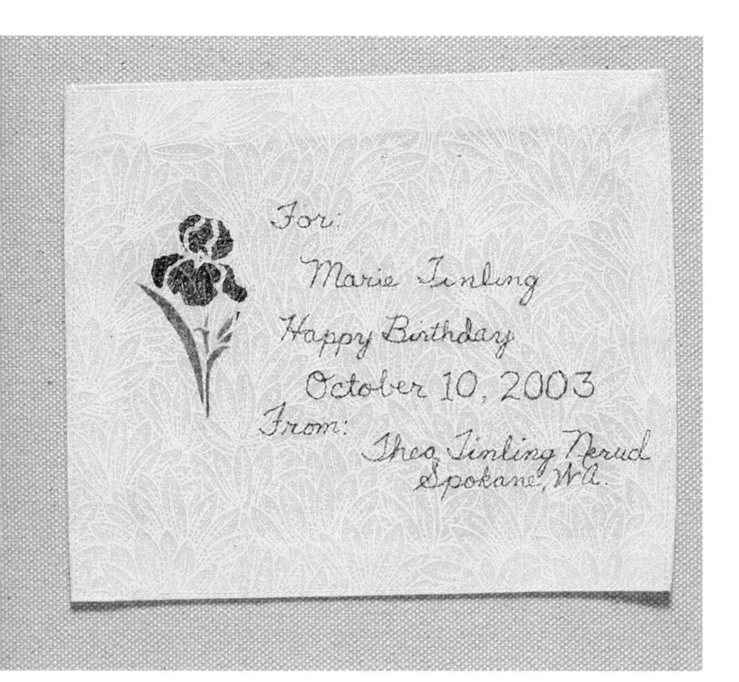

Dimensions: 6" x 5"
Hand-inked lettering. To learn more about stenciled designs, see page 77.

Materials

- Light-colored, closely woven cotton fabric such as Pimatex, for the label and for practicing
- Freezer paper
- Heavy permanent black marker
- Straightedge or ruler
- Iron
- Fine-point permanent markers such as Pigma Micron or Sanford Sharpie Ultra-Fine Point pens
- Masking tape (optional)
- Light table or window (optional)

Lettering the Label

1. Using the heavy black marker, outline the desired shape of your label on the freezer paper. Remember, labels do not have to be rectangular! For this example, we'll use a circle. Using the heavy marker and the straightedge or ruler, draw lettering guidelines on the uncoated side of the freezer paper.

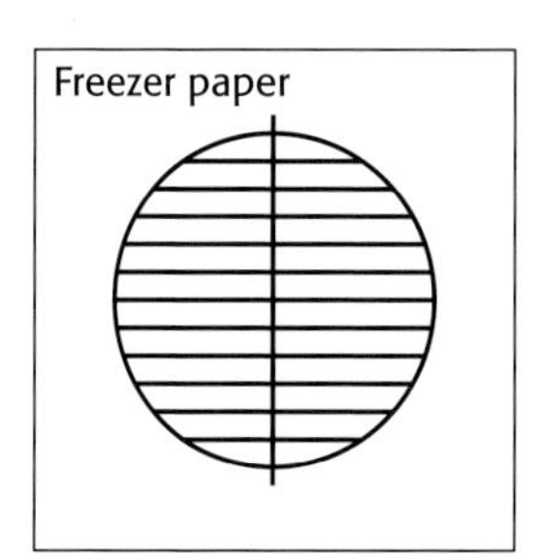

Lettering Guide for a Circular Label

2. Using a medium-hot iron, press the shiny side of the freezer paper to the wrong side of the label fabric, leaving at least ¼" of fabric extending past the freezer paper on all sides.
3. With the fine-point permanent markers, practice lettering on scraps of fabric backed with freezer paper. If you want to decorate your label, try adding simple designs around the edges, like the ones shown below.

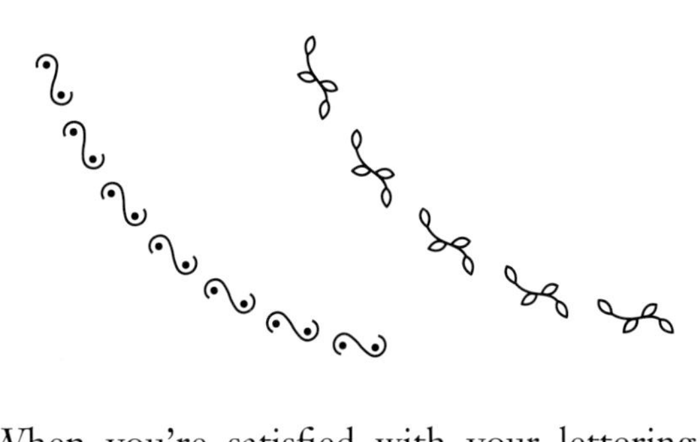

4. When you're satisfied with your lettering and any design elements, start marking your prepared fabric label. (If you have trouble seeing the lettering guidelines through the fabric, use masking tape to attach the label to a window or place the label on a light table.) After you finish marking, cut the fabric around the shape marked on the freezer paper, maintaining a ¼" seam allowance.

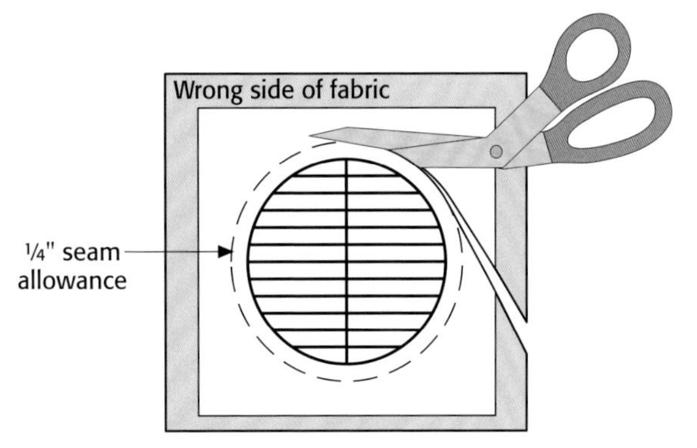

5. Remove freezer paper. Press the label. Turn under the edges and attach the label to the back of the quilt.

Traced Lettering

If you don't like the way your freehand lettering looks, try tracing printed lettering. To see the printed letters through the fabric, place the printed text beneath the fabric and tape both layers to a light table or window. Using a fine-point permanent marker, trace the lettering onto the fabric.

I make an inexpensive light table by opening my dining room table and placing a sheet of glass across the opening where the extension leaf would go. A table lamp without a shade, placed on the floor, provides the light.

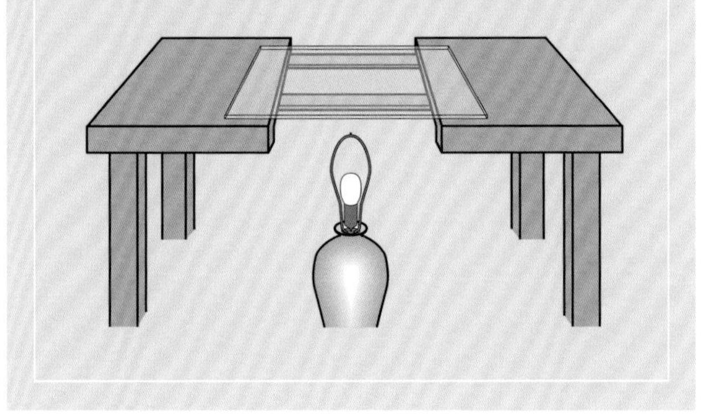

CRAYON LETTERING

WAX CRAYONS can be used on fabric for lettering and drawings. This is a natural for children's projects.

DIMENSIONS: 10" x 7½"
Crayon-lettered label

Materials

- Light-colored fabric for label
- Freezer paper
- Black permanent marker
- Straightedge or ruler
- Wax crayons
- Terrycloth towel
- Brown paper grocery bags
- Iron

Lettering the Label

1. Cut the label fabric and freezer paper to the desired shape and size, including ¼" seam allowances.
2. Compose your text. Using the permanent marker and the straightedge or ruler, mark text guidelines on the uncoated side of the freezer paper. Press the shiny side of the freezer paper to the wrong side of the label fabric.
3. Using firm pressure on the crayons, mark the text and any design elements on the right side of the label. Remove the freezer paper.
4. Place a terrycloth towel on an ironing board. Position the label on top of the towel, right side up. Avoiding any printed areas, cut a piece of paper from a grocery bag, making sure the piece is large enough to cover the label. Position the paper over the label.
5. Test the temperature of your iron on scrap fabric—it needs to be as hot as possible without scorching the fabric. To set the crayon design, press the paper on top of the label with the hot iron. The excess wax will be absorbed into the paper. Be careful not to touch the hot iron directly to the crayon marks, because the wax will adhere to your iron. If the paper shifts as you press, position a new or a clean piece over the label to avoid smearing your design.

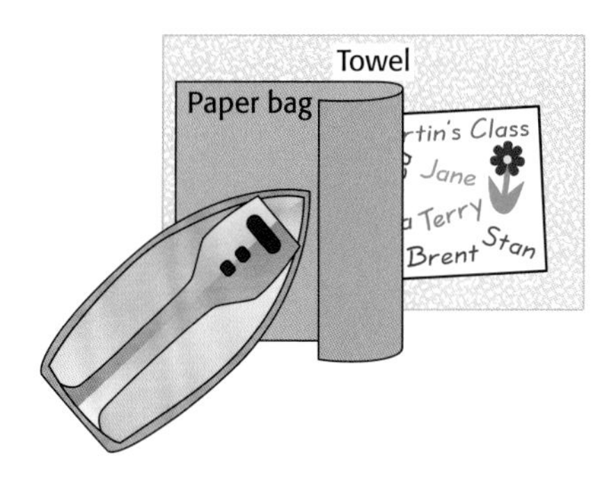

6. Turn under the edges of the label and stitch it to the back of the quilt.

Embroidered Lettering

DEPENDING ON THE method and design, embroidered lettering can have handcrafted appeal or professional-looking polish.

HAND-EMBROIDERED LETTERING

IF YOU like hand quilting, you might also enjoy hand embroidering your quilt labels. Many old quilts are signed in this manner, and the lettering is very durable.

Hand-embroidered lettering

Materials

- Fabric for label
- Embroidery floss
- Embroidery needle
- Freezer paper
- Pencil or air-soluble fabric marker

Lettering the Label

1. Cut the freezer paper into the approximate size and shape of your label. Using an iron set on medium heat, press the shiny side of the freezer paper to the wrong side of the label fabric.
2. Using the pencil or air-soluble marker, write the label lettering on the fabric. Make sure that you write larger than you normally would, so that you will be able to embroider the words easily.
3. Remove the freezer paper. Using two strands of embroidery floss, backstitch over the lettering.

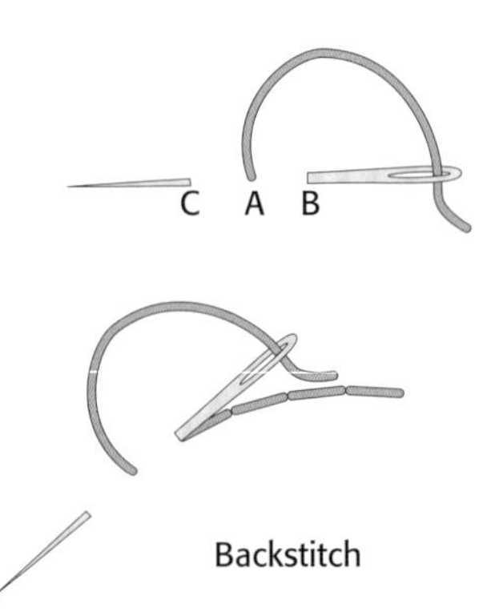

MACHINE-EMBROIDERED LETTERING

MANY SEWING and embroidery machines have lettering functions. Some can do everything but sing the national anthem! To investigate the capabilities of your machine, refer to your manual and visit your local dealership. Experiment with various stitches to see how many different looks you can create.

My nearest quilt shop regularly schedules "Make It and Take It" classes so that customers can try out embroidery machines. Check local quilt shops for similar workshops. As with all tools, embroidery machines seem to get "smarter" the longer you use them, so spend some time practicing before making an important label.

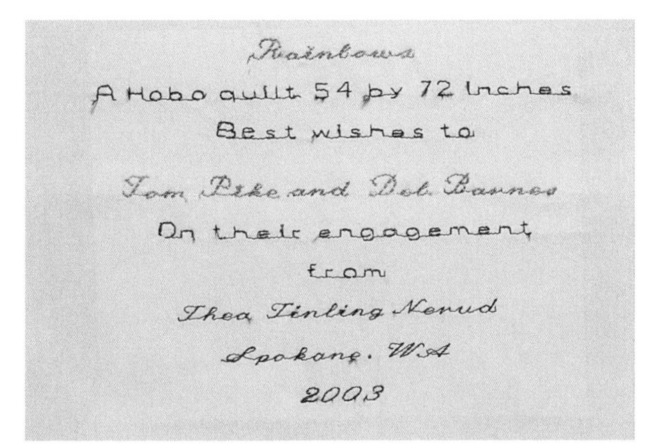

DIMENSIONS: 6½" x 5"
My first machine-embroidered label. The lettering was done on a Bernina Artista 200.

DIMENSIONS: 10" x 4"

On the cat label shown above, Karen Buck machine embroidered the lettering and hand embroidered the face, using fabric appliqués for the eyes.

If you'd like this cat to peer from your label, use the pattern below. Make templates for the eyes, tracing the ovals onto yellow fabric and the pupils onto black. Cut out the eyes and then machine satin stitch the black pupils onto the yellow ovals. Position the eyes on your label fabric and satin stitch them in place. Hand embroider the nose, mouth, and whiskers.

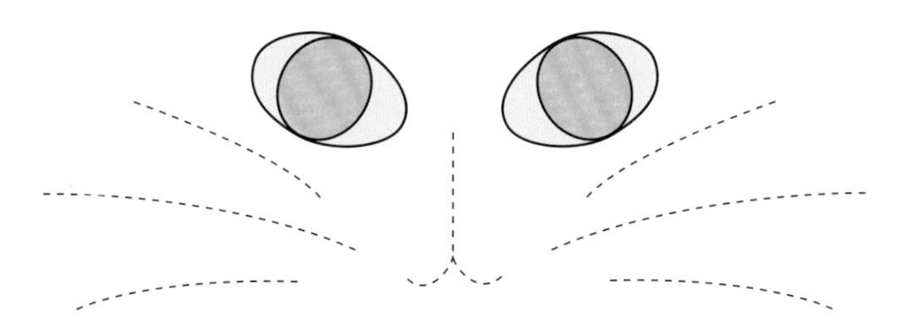

PAPER-PIECED CAT

DIMENSIONS: 6¼" x 8¼"

This machine-embroidered label by Karen Buck includes a little paper-pieced cat for decoration. The name on the label is that of a fictional quiltmaker from *The Crematory Cat*, one of Karen's Killer Quilts mysteries.

Materials

- Assorted scraps of fabric for cat and background area
- 2½" x 40" strip of light blue fabric
- Thread to contrast cat fabric
- Fine-point permanent marker
- Tracing paper
- Freezer paper

Making the Label

Follow these steps to create a label with a paper-pieced cat at the center.

1. Using the fine-point permanent marker, trace the cat design from page 14 onto tracing paper, copying all solid and dashed lines but those for the tail. Include the lines for seam allowances.

2. On the wrong side of the traced cat pattern, place a scrap of background fabric on top of piece 1, with the right side of the fabric facing up. Make sure that at least ¼" of the fabric scrap extends beyond the seam lines on all sides of piece 1.

3. Place a scrap of cat fabric over the line between pieces 1 and 2, with the right side facing *down*. Make sure that piece 2 is large enough that at least ¼" of fabric will extend beyond the seam lines on all sides of piece 2 after the seam has been stitched.

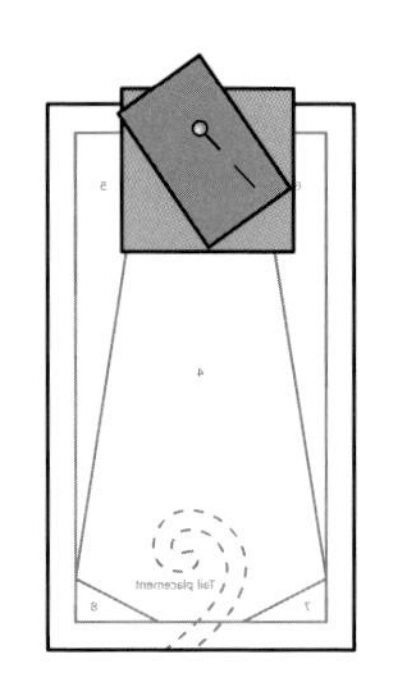

4. Flip the pattern so that the tracing paper is facing up and the fabric is underneath. Using a short machine stitch (10 to 12 stitches per inch), sew on the line between pieces 1 and 2. Remove the piece from the machine, open the fabric, and finger-press the seam. Trim any excess seam allowance to ¼". Double-check to make sure that at least ¼" of fabric extends beyond the seam lines on all sides of piece 2.

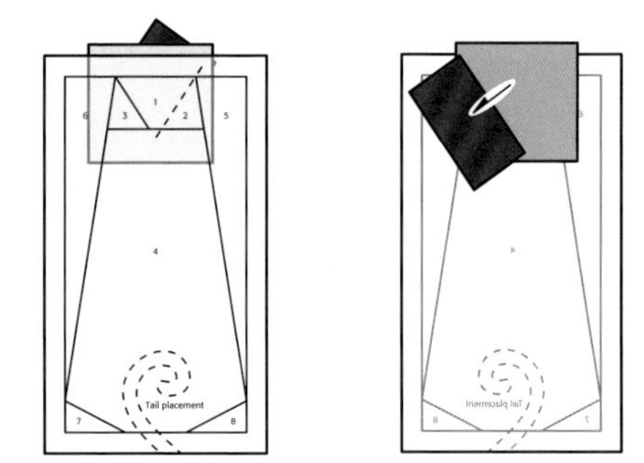

5. Continue sewing pieces 3–8 in the same manner. Press the completed paper-pieced cat.

6. Trace the tail onto freezer paper. Cut out the tail shape on the marked line. With the shiny side down, press the tail onto the front of the paper-pieced cat, making sure the base of the tail will be caught in the bottom seam. Using the contrasting thread, machine topstitch around the edges of the paper tail. Remove the paper from the cat.

7. Sew 2½"-wide strips of fabric to the sides of the paper-pieced cat. Trim the ends of the strips even with the top and bottom edges. Repeat to sew 2½"-wide strips of fabric to the top and bottom of the paper-pieced cat.

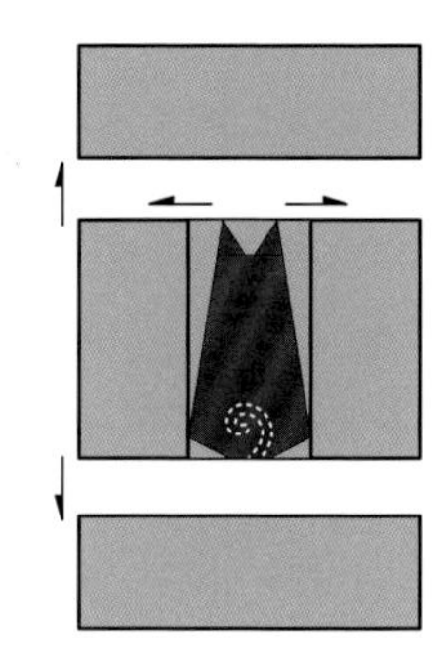

8. Machine embroider the desired lettering. Press the completed label. If desired, trim the edges with pinking shears. Attach the label to your quilt.

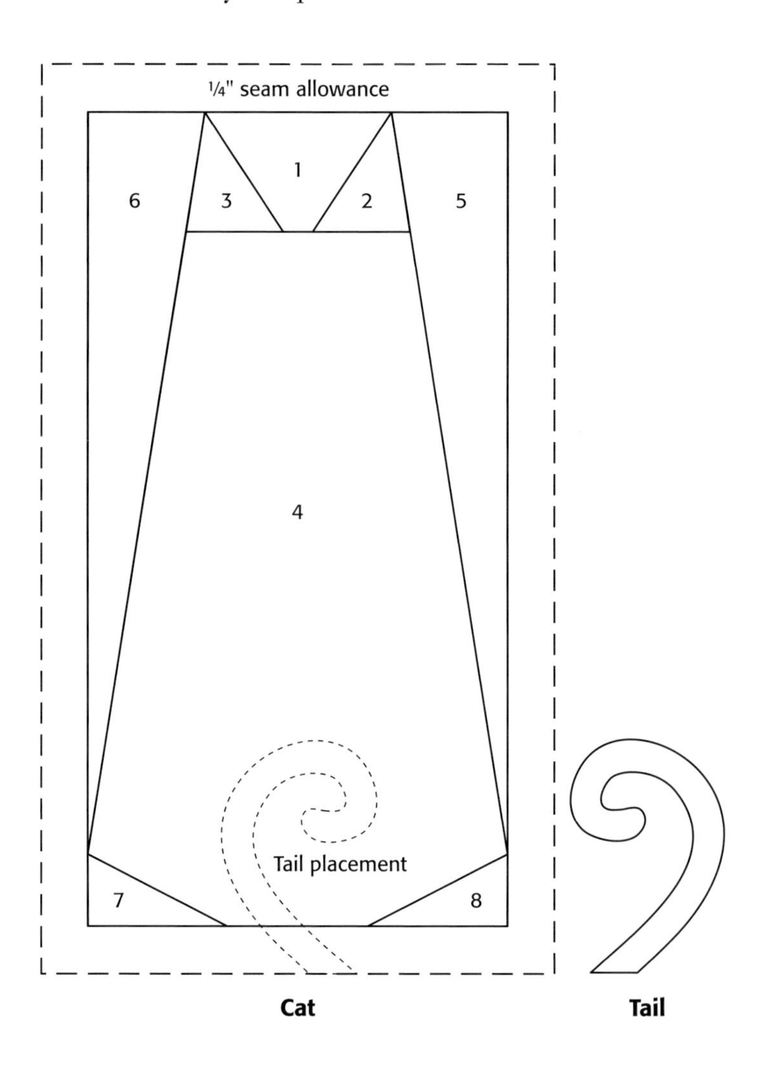

Cross-Stitched Lettering

On even-weave fabric, counted cross-stitch designs with backstitched lettering make beautiful labels.

EVEN-WEAVE FABRIC

Fabrics like Aida cloth have an even number of squares per inch both horizontally and vertically, making it easy and fun to work from charted alphabets.

Dimensions: 8" x 3"
Cross-stitched label with backstitched lettering in variegated floss

Materials

- 14-count Aida cloth in cream or pink
- Embroidery floss in white, variegated medium rose, variegated dark rose, and variegated teal
- Basting thread
- Graph paper and pencil
- Masking tape
- Tapestry needle
- Anti-fray fluid

Making the Label

Follow these steps to create a cross-stitched label with a cactus flower at one side.

1. Compose your text. On a piece of graph paper, mark horizontal and vertical center lines. Chart the lettering on the graph paper, using the alphabet on page 16. Count each square as one stitch.
2. Cut a piece of Aida cloth at least 1" larger than the size of your finished label. For example, if you want your label to measure 3⅛" x 8" after you've turned under seam allowances, you'd cut the Aida cloth to 4⅛" x 9".
3. Fold a piece of masking tape over each edge of the cloth to prevent fraying. Baste a straight line through the horizontal center of the fabric. Then baste through the vertical center of the cactus flower area and the vertical center of the lettering area.

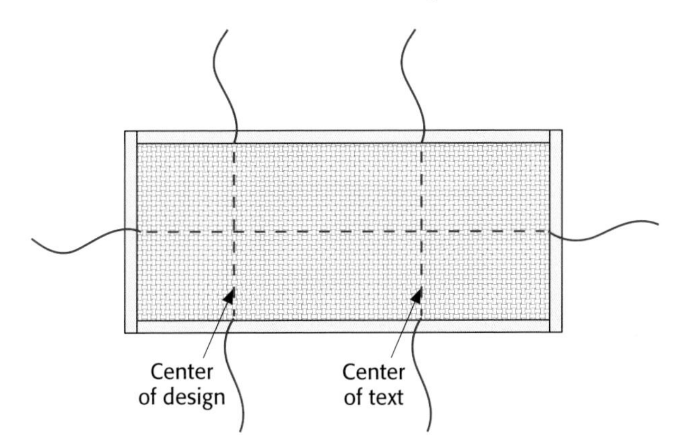

4. Using two strands of floss, cross-stitch the cactus flower design shown at right, matching the center lines of the design to the basting threads. Stitch the lettering, using a backstitch (page 12) and following the alphabet chart at right.

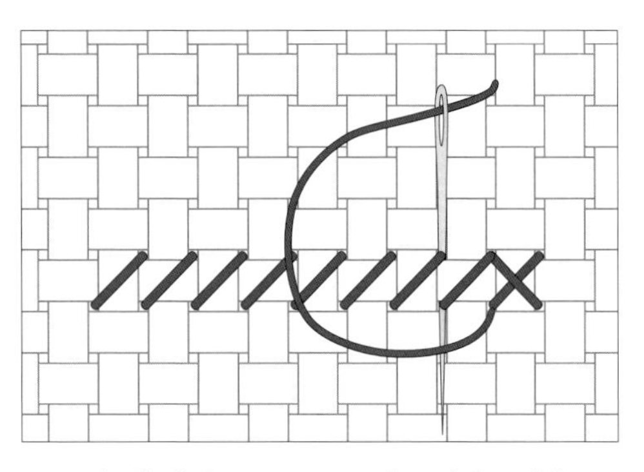

Work all stitches across row from left to right; then work stitches from right to left.

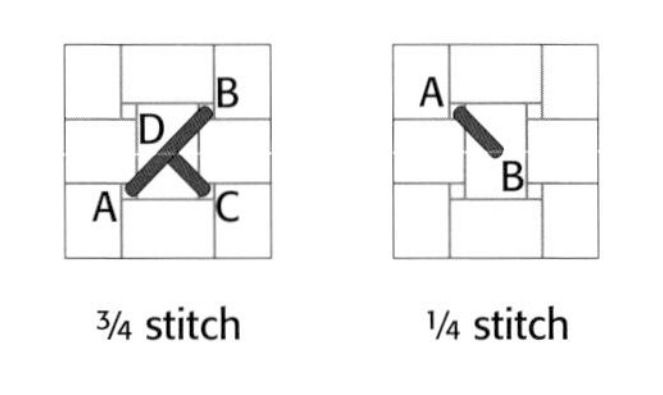

¾ stitch ¼ stitch

5. Remove the tape and basting threads. Trim the cloth to the desired size, maintaining a ¼" seam allowance. Apply anti-fray fluid to the edges and allow to dry. Hand wash the label using a mild detergent. Lay the label on a terrycloth towel and pin it in place to shape it. Allow to dry.

6. Press the finished label. Turn under the edges and stitch the label to the back of the quilt.

Backstitch Alphabet

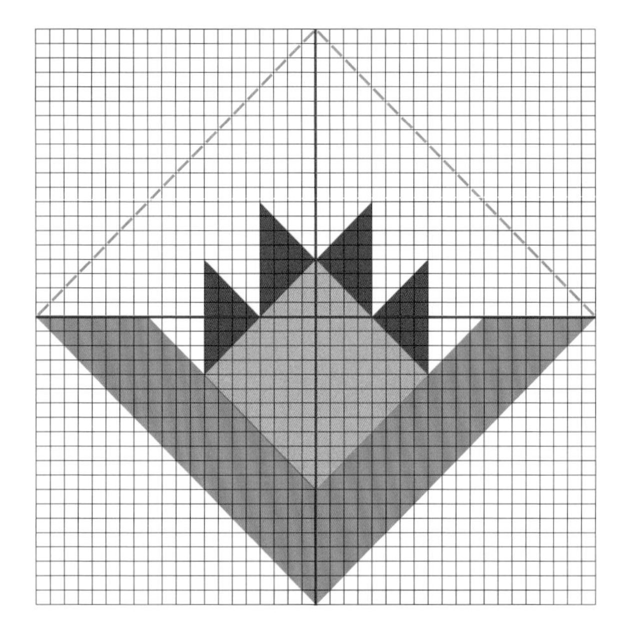

Cactus Flower Cross-Stitch Chart

Aida 14 count
1 square = 1 stitch
Stitch area 40 x 40, 2¼" x 2¼"

Stitch Key

Cross-stitch	¾ stitch	¼ stitch	Backstitch
White		◩	
Variegated medium rose		◩	
Variegated dark rose	◩		
Variegated teal	◩		◩

WASTE CANVAS

You can do counted cross-stitch on any fabric by using waste canvas, a grid of stiff threads that have been coated with sizing to keep them securely in position, as a guide.

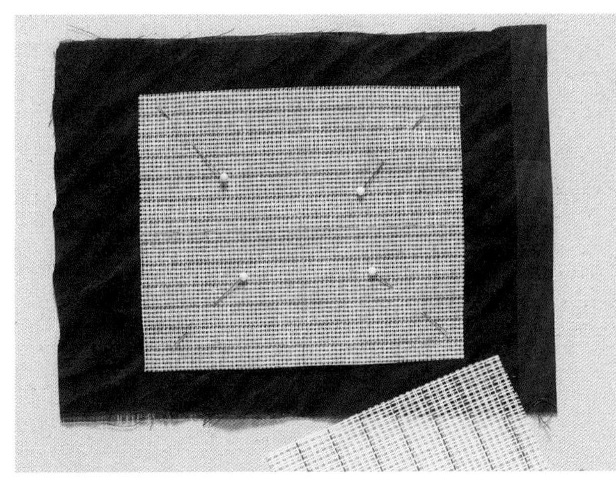

Waste canvas pinned to label fabric

Dimensions: 5½" x 5½"
Finished label after removal of waste canvas strands

Materials

- Fabric for label
- Waste canvas
- Fusible interfacing or fusible stabilizer
- Embroidery floss
- Basting thread
- Graph paper and pencil
- Sharp embroidery needle
- Permanent marker
- Tweezers or forceps

Making the Label

Follow these steps to make a cross-stitched label by using waste canvas.

1. Compose your text. Mark vertical and horizontal center lines on a piece of graph paper. Chart the lettering on the graph paper, using the alphabet on page 16. Count each square as one stitch.
2. Cut the fusible interfacing or stabilizer and the waste canvas 1" larger than the finished label. Cut the label fabric to the same size and shape. Press the fusible interfacing or stabilizer to the back of the label fabric. Using the permanent marker, draw vertical and horizontal center lines on the waste canvas and then baste the canvas to the front of the label fabric.
3. Using two strands of floss and covering two threads of waste canvas for each stitch, work the lettering and the border design shown below. The embroidery needle needs to be sharp enough to stitch through all layers of the waste canvas, label fabric, and interfacing or stabilizer.

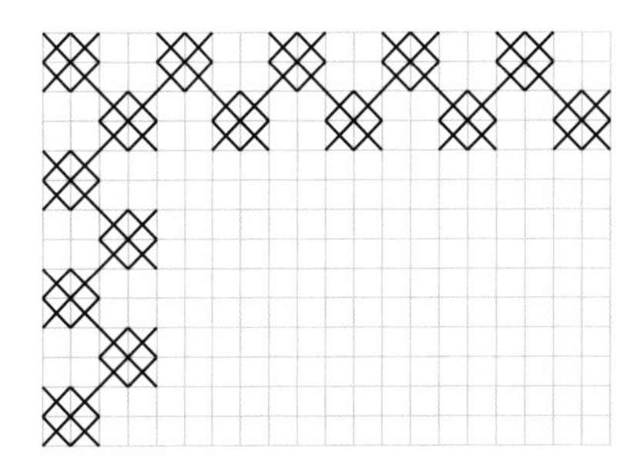

Cross-Stitch Checkered Border

4. When you've finished stitching the lettering and border design, wet the waste canvas to dissolve the sizing. Use tweezers or forceps to remove the canvas strands, leaving just the stitching on the label fabric. Let the fabric dry and then press the label. Turn under the edges and attach the label to the back of the quilt.

Enlarging Patterns

In this book you'll find instructions for making labels of particular sizes. You might want to adjust some of the patterns to accommodate your lettering requirements. First compose your label, and then determine how large your lettered fabric needs to be. To figure out how much a pattern needs to be enlarged or reduced, divide the measurement you need the pattern to be by the original size. Move the decimal point in the resulting number two places to the right to make the number a percentage. For example, if the lettering area of a label measures 2½" tall and you want your finished label to measure 3½" tall, divide 3½" by 2½". The answer is 1.4. Move the decimal point two places to the right (140), and you'll know you need to enlarge the original pattern by 140%. Use a photocopy machine to enlarge any pattern pieces to the size you need. If necessary, you can enlarge your first enlargement to create an even larger pattern.

If you don't have access to a photocopy machine, you can use the grid method. Trace the original pattern onto tracing paper and fold or draw a grid over the design, dividing the pattern into halves, quarters, or eighths. After determining how large you need a pattern piece to be, draw another grid on paper that is the size of the required pattern piece. Use the same number of lines in each grid and divide the design area horizontally and vertically into halves, quarters, or eighths. Draw the same shape in each new grid square that you see in the original pattern's corresponding grid square.

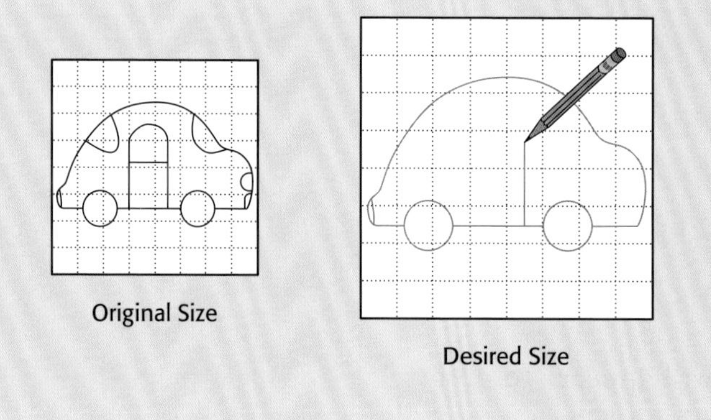

Computer Lettering

COMPUTER LETTERING IS my favorite labeling technique. Anything you can print from your computer you can print onto fabric. Computer lettering allows you to include more text in less space than hand lettering or embroidery.

Computers make it easy to experiment, because you can view layouts onscreen and print samples on plain paper before printing onto iron-on transfer film or printable fabric. Try various font styles, from fancy to plain, and different point sizes, from tiny to huge. Center each line of text or make the margins justified on both sides. If you want to make multiple labels from a single printing, try fitting multiple text blocks into two or three columns. Add borders around your messages with your word processor's drawing tools. Switch the page orientation from portrait (vertical) to landscape (horizontal). Vary the widths of the margins.

New products for using fabric with printers are coming on the market all the time. Be sure to read all of the instructions on any that you use. To avoid nasty surprises, make sure to follow the washing instructions exactly as directed. Some products will not withstand washing and others require special care.

Make sure you know how to load paper into your printer. You need to know which end of the paper will become the top of the page and on which side the printing will appear. To do a test, write the words "front" and "top" on a piece of paper where you think the front and top would be on a printed page. Run the paper through your printer and see if you were right about the positioning. My HP printer feeds paper in top first and face down, while my Canon, Lexmark, and Epson printers feed the paper top first and face up.

Reversing Text

In addition to knowing how to properly load transfer film or printable fabric into your printer, you'll need to know how to instruct your machine to print reversed (mirror-image) text. First, familiarize yourself with your printer's Print dialog box.

1. With your word-processing program open, select Print from the File menu.
2. Select your printer.
3. Select Properties.

Next, you'll need to do a bit of exploring within this Properties page. Either on the first screen, or on a screen you'll see when you click one of the "tabs" at the top of the page, you may find a term such as reverse printing, mirror image, flip vertical, or flip horizontal. If you see such an option, select it and proceed to print. On the other hand, some printer software will automatically reverse the text when you go to the Paper or Specialty Paper choice and select iron-on transfer, T-shirt transfer, or back print film.

Check the User Guide and Help in your printer software, if available. Sometimes you just have to try things and practice first. Don't be intimidated; think of this as a chance to get better acquainted with your printer and its many possibilities!

I initially tried to compile short, specific instructions about reversed printing for each major brand of printer, but this proved impossible—I came across too many inconsistencies, not only across different operating systems but even in the directions within each product line. Instead, check your printer manufacturer's Web site for information. If you select your printer model at the appropriate site, you can locate more specific instructions under "Documentation," or you can email a company's tech-support folks under "Contact Us" or "Support."

IRON-ON TRANSFER FILM

IRON-ON TRANSFER film is a paper-backed transfer material that can be used with an ink-jet printer. There are at least two types. One is a clear transfer film for use on light fabrics and is usually marketed as an "iron-on transfer" or "T-shirt transfer." The other type is an opaque white transfer film on which you can print dark lettering, and it's generally referred to as a "dark-fabric iron-on transfer." Both types press onto fabric, but the printing and pressing techniques are different. If your local quilt shop doesn't carry these products, try an office-supply store.

IRON-ON TRANSFERS FOR LIGHT FABRIC

Work through the following instructions to make an iron-on label for light fabric.

DIMENSIONS: 8" x 8"
The lettering for this label was applied with clear iron-on transfer film.

Materials for Light Fabrics

- Light-colored cotton fabric with smooth finish for label
- Clear iron-on transfer film
- Iron emptied of water
- Two pieces of muslin or a smooth pillowcase
- Hard surface that can withstand heat, such as a wooden cutting board or breadboard. Do not use a glass or metal surface or an ironing board.
- Scissors for trimming transfer film

Making a Light-Fabric Transfer Label

1. Using a computer, compose your text. Format your document with ½" margins at the top, bottom, and sides of the page to take advantage of as much label space as possible. Print a test sample of the text on plain paper to check the size, layout, and spelling.
2. Convert the text to a reverse, or mirror, image, referring to "Reversing Text" on page 19 as needed.
3. Following the manufacturer's instructions, print the text onto the clear transfer film. Allow the printed transfer film to dry; do not handle the transfer film while the ink is still wet.
4. Preheat your iron on the cotton setting for at least eight minutes. Following the transfer manufacturer's instructions, test the iron on scraps of fabric and transfer film. The temperature needs to be high enough to make the transfer film adhere without causing any scorching.
5. Place two layers of muslin or a smooth pillowcase on the hard surface. Place your label fabric right side up on top, and press it with the iron to preheat the fabric and remove excess moisture and wrinkles.

6. Trim away any blank areas of transfer film around the lettering, cutting smooth curves and leaving an area from ¼" to ½" wide at one side. Fold over the extra film to make a peeling handle, as shown.

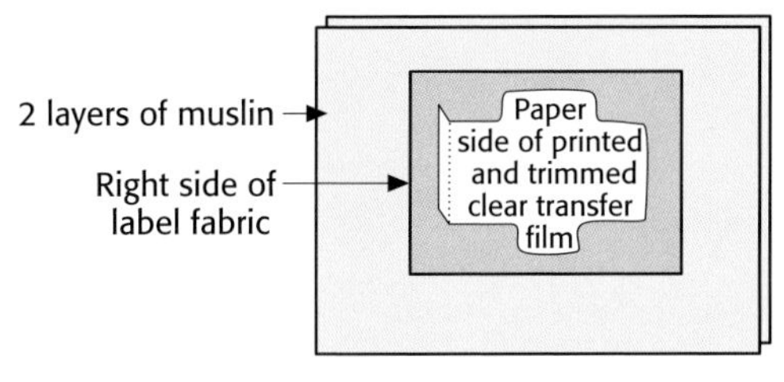

Fold up ¼" of the transfer film to make a peeling handle.

7. Place the transfer film facedown on the label fabric. Press, using heavy pressure and sliding the iron over the transfer film until it sticks to the fabric. This usually takes from 60 to 90 seconds. Make sure to press all areas *except* the folded peeling handle.
8. Wait three to five seconds and then grasp the peeling handle, removing the paper backing in a smooth, even motion.

Handling a Light-Fabric Transfer

After removing the paper backing, never iron directly on top of a transferred image. If you do, it will melt. You can place a sheet of baking parchment over the image and press for a few seconds at medium heat without damaging the transfer.

Iron-On Transfers for Dark Fabric

Work through the following instructions to make an iron-on label for dark fabric.

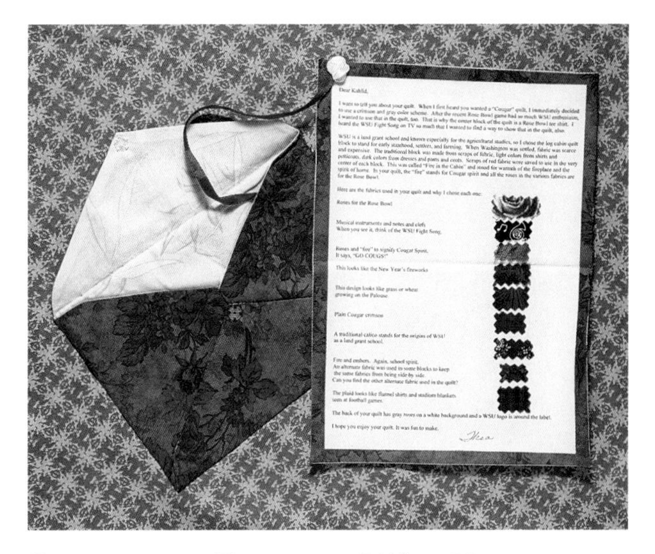

Dimensions: Envelope 7½" x 5", Card 6¾" x 9½"
This letter, applied with dark-fabric iron-on transfer film, shows up well against the dark background fabric. Swatches of each of the quilt fabrics are attached, along with the reason that each fabric was chosen.

Materials for Dark Fabrics

- Dark-colored cotton fabric with smooth finish for label
- Iron-on transfer film for dark fabric
- Silicone ironing sheet (included with iron-on transfer film)
- Iron emptied of water
- Two pieces of muslin or a smooth pillowcase
- Hard surface that can withstand heat, such as a wooden cutting board or breadboard. Do not use a glass or metal surface or an ironing board.
- Scissors for trimming transfer film

Making a Dark-Fabric Transfer Label

1. Using a computer, compose your text. Format your document with ½" margins at the top, bottom, and sides of the page to take advantage of as much of the label space as possible. Print a test sample of the text on plain paper to check the size, layout, and spelling.
2. Following the manufacturer's instructions, print the text onto the dark-fabric transfer film. Choose a printer setting that will not use high levels of ink. Do *not* create a reverse, or mirror, image of the text for this method. Allow the printed transfer film to dry; do not handle the transfer film while the ink is still wet.
3. Preheat your iron for at least eight minutes on the cotton setting. Following the transfer manufacturer's instructions, test the iron on scraps of fabric and transfer film. The temperature needs to be high enough to make the transfer film adhere without causing any scorching.
4. Place two layers of muslin or a smooth pillowcase on the hard surface. Place your label fabric right side up on top, and press with the iron to preheat the fabric and remove excess moisture and wrinkles.
5. Trim the printed label to a nice shape. The transfer background will show on your finished label, so make sure that the lettering is centered, the margins are even, and the edges are smooth.
6. Carefully remove the paper backing from the transfer film and discard it. Position the text face up on the label fabric. Place the silicone ironing sheet included with the transfer film on top of the transfer. Using medium-firm pressure, slide the iron constantly over the ironing sheet to adhere the transfer to the fabric. Make sure to run the iron completely over the edges of the image.

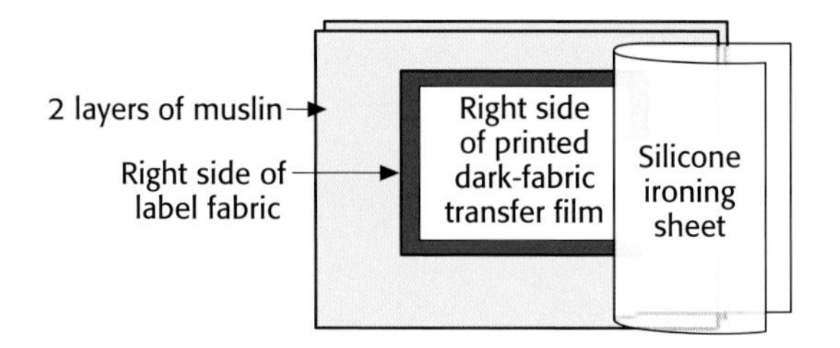

Handling a Dark-Fabric Transfer

Never iron directly on top of a transferred image or it will melt. You also have to be careful not to overheat a transfer when ironing from the wrong side of the fabric. You can place the silicone sheet over the transfer and press at medium heat for a few seconds without damaging the transfer.

PRINTABLE FABRIC

Creating beautiful quilt labels is fast and easy when you use fabric that's been pretreated for use with an ink-jet printer (not laser printers). You can buy paper-backed, colorfast fabric sheets that will easily feed through an ink-jet printer, or you can make your own. With printable fabric, you just create a computer document, print it, and then attach the printed label to a quilt.

I had thrifty grandmothers who passed that trait on to me. I can make my own colorfast fabric at a fraction of the cost of commercial ready-to-print fabric, and I'm willing to trade some of my time for the lower cost. Making my own printable fabric also gives me the option of using light- to medium-value colors rather than just white or cream, which are the only printable-fabric colors currently available for purchase.

When using commercial printable fabric, follow the manufacturer's instructions for washing and pressing. Homemade printable fabric can be washed and pressed after printing.

Materials for Making Printable Fabric

To make labels with the treated fabric, you'll need access to a computer and an ink-jet printer. Refer to your word processor's help files and your printer manual as needed.

- 42"-wide, prewashed, closely woven 100% cotton such as Pimatex (or silk)
- 18"-wide freezer paper
- Rotary cutter (fitted with an old blade for cutting paper)
- Cutting mat and ruler
- Bubble Jet Set 2000*
- Bubble Jet Rinse
- Flat pan for soaking fabric
- Basin for hand washing fabric
- Iron

**Visit www.cjenkinscompany.com if you'd like to learn more about Bubble Jet products and compatible printers.*

Making and Lettering Printable Fabric

1. Using a rotary cutter, mat, and ruler, cut the fabric and freezer paper to a size that will go through your printer, usually 8½" x 11". I cut 11" strips of both fabric and paper and then crosscut them into 8½" widths. From a 42"-wide strip of Pimatex cotton this yields five sheets of fabric (but only four sheets from a narrower fabric or from a fabric with wide selvages). You can get two sheets per 18"-wide strip of freezer paper.

2. Pour Bubble Jet Set solution into a flat pan. I use a rectangular plastic washbasin that my fabric pieces can lie flat in. Saturate the fabric in the solution for five minutes. To avoid wrinkles and uneven penetration of the solution, don't wring out the fabric. I like to spread my fabric on a countertop, smooth out the wrinkles, and allow it to air dry. You can also let it drip-dry or dry on a towel. Pour any leftover solution back into the bottle and recap it tightly. Once opened, Bubble Jet Set has a shelf life of one year.

3. Press the dry, treated fabric pieces to the shiny side of the freezer-paper pieces. Either use the fabric immediately or store it in a sealed, two-gallon plastic bag, which will keep the fabric ready to use for months. (*Note:* If you live in an area with high humidity, you might not be able to successfully store treated fabric for later use.)

4. Compose your label on a computer. Place a sheet of paper-backed fabric in an ink-jet printer so that the printing will appear on the fabric side. Print your label. Allow the ink to dry for at least 30 minutes. Remove the freezer paper. (You can reuse a sheet of freezer paper several times until it no longer adheres evenly to fabric.)

5. Using four capfuls of Bubble Jet Rinse per gallon of cold water, hand wash the printed fabric for two minutes in a basin. Wash one sheet at a time so that excess ink or fabric dye won't transfer from one sheet to another. Do not wring out the fabric. Discard the wash water when it becomes discolored.

6. Rinse the fabric in cold water and allow it to drip-dry, or air-dry it on a towel. For faster results, you can blow-dry the fabric with a hairdryer.

7. Attach the printed label to your project.

Adding Photos to Labels

A PHOTO OF the quiltmaker, recipient, or other special person makes a wonderful addition to a quilt label. If you don't have a computer, you can simply use photo-transfer paper and a color laser copier to create a permanent, iron-on transfer (see "Working with Photo-Transfer Products" at right). As an alternative, some copy shops will scan photos and print them onto printable fabric or sheets of iron-on transfer paper for you. Look under "Photocopying and Duplication Services" or "Printers" in the Yellow Pages and call to ask about prices. If you're uncomfortable with the cost, you may decide to use a friend's or the public library's computer equipment instead.

For quiltmakers who are planning to use a computer, the biggest problem is usually getting photos from a camera into the computer. For a nominal cost, film-processing labs will put photos onto a floppy disk or CD when you have your film developed. Some will even put them on the Internet, so that you can download them into your computer at home.

Once you have a photo file, you might want to alter the size or enhance the image. Photo-editing software ranges from simple, user-friendly features built into word-processing programs to extremely complex, specialized programs with steep learning curves. My printer and scanner software allow me to do most of the photo editing I need to do, and my digital camera's memory card fits right into a slot on my printer so that I can download photos into my computer. My life partner, Norman, uses Adobe PhotoShop to correct flaws in old photos (a task that many photo-processing labs will perform for you), and he saves photos in the size I need. In this book, most of the photos on the labels measure 3" x 3".

Whatever software you plan to use, practice scanning, editing, saving, and printing photos on plain paper before printing photos on expensive printable fabric or iron-on transfer film.

WORKING WITH PHOTO-TRANSFER PRODUCTS

THERE ARE a number of ways to get photos onto fabric. More and more photo-transfer products and services are becoming available. Some methods can withstand washing after copying, some can't. Check the packaging carefully before you buy.

Iron-On Transfer Paper and a Color Laser Copier: Transfer products such as That Patchwork Place Photo-Transfer Paper allow you to copy an image onto paper with a color laser copier and then iron that image onto fabric for a permanent, ironable, washable bond.

Printable Fabric and an Ink-Jet Printer: You can print photos onto fabric by using an ink-jet printer and the fabrics discussed in "Printable Fabric" on page 22.

COMBINING PHOTOS WITH CAPTIONS

YOU'VE PROBABLY seen wonderful memory quilts featuring beautiful, old photos. Most of the ones I've seen haven't included photo captions. I think that photos on quilts are much more meaningful if names of people and places, dates, and occasions are given along with the photos.

Word-processing and photo-editing programs allow you to combine text and photos and print them from your computer. Or, if you plan to have photos scanned at a copy shop, you can type or handwrite captions for each photo on plain paper, cut them out, and then lay each caption on the scanner with the photo. The same method works for color laser copies made with photo-transfer paper.

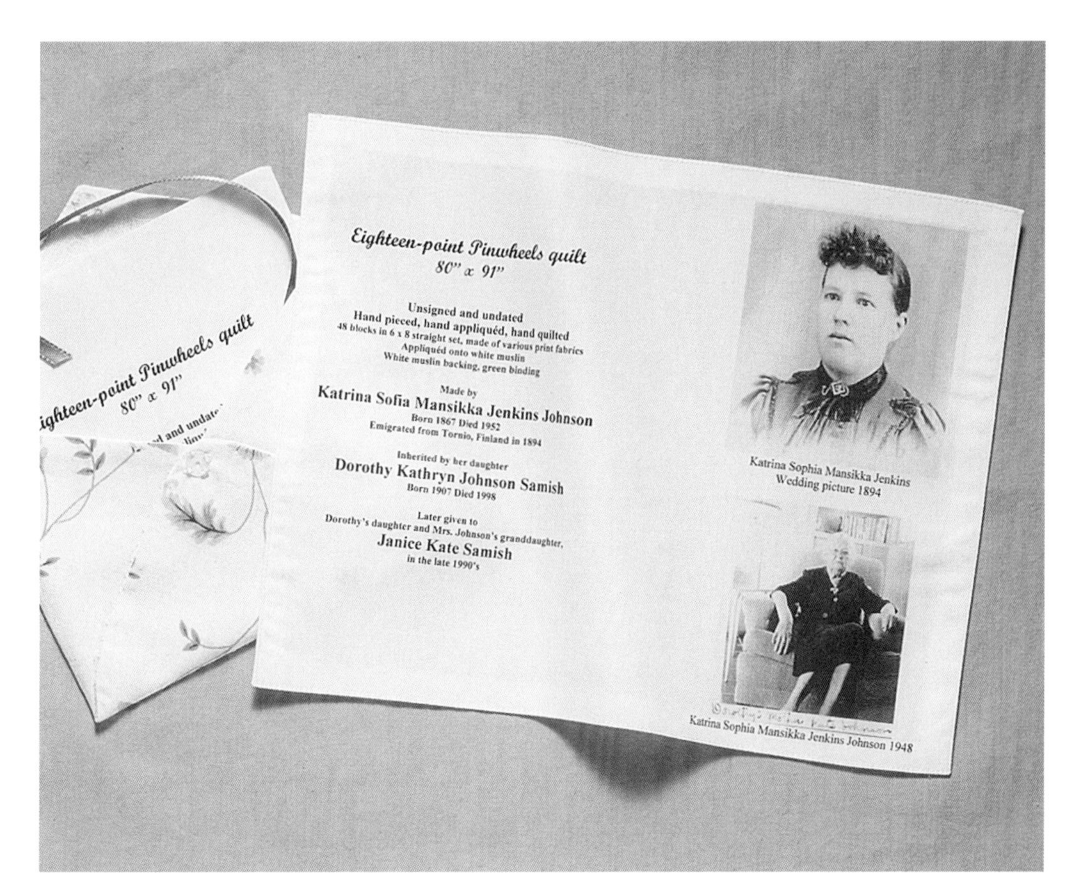

DIMENSIONS: ENVELOPE 5½" x 4½", CARD 10" x 7½"

For this label, old photographs were scanned into a computer and resized. Scratches on the photos were corrected in Adobe PhotoShop, and then the images were inserted into a Microsoft Word document so that captions could be added.

Labels for Special Circumstances

To CHOOSE THE best style and format for a label, consider the size and type of item you want to label, and think about the amount of information you want to include. Consider the following types of labels and see which ones will best suit your needs.

QUILT-SHOW LABELS

MOST QUILT shows require that a label be sewn to the back of each quilt, with the maker's name, address, and phone number on it, preferably in large, easy-to-read lettering. The following steps will give you four quilt-show labels per 8½" x 11" sheet of printable fabric or iron-on transfer film.

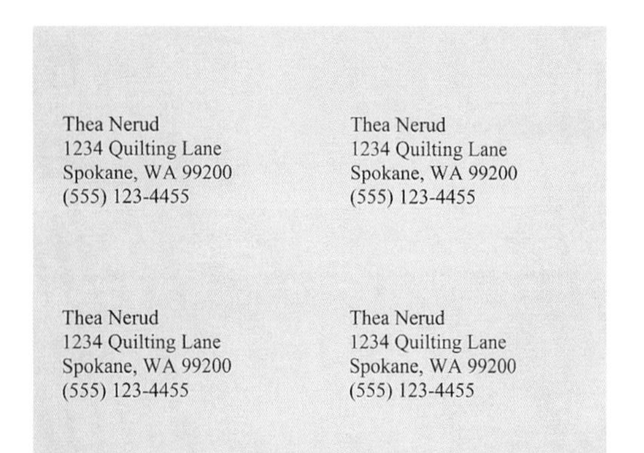

DIMENSIONS: 8½" x 11"
Four labels on a sheet of homemade printer fabric. Note the crisp lettering you can achieve by printing on cotton with a high thread count.

Materials

- You'll need access to a computer and an ink-jet printer. Refer to your word processor's help files and your printer manual as needed.
- Printable fabric ***or*** untreated, light- to medium-value cotton fabric and clear iron-on transfer film (see "Iron-on Transfer Film" on page 20).

Making the Labels

Follow these steps to make multiple quilt-show labels.

1. Open a new, blank document in your word-processing program and save it as "My Quilt-Show Labels."
2. Set the page size for letter (8½" x 11") and the margins to ½" at the top, bottom, and sides. Choose the landscape (horizontal) page orientation and set up a two-column format. Select either flush left or center justification for the text. Choose a font you like and a large point size—I use boldface Times New Roman at 26-point size.
3. Type your name on the first line. On the line below, type your street address. On the third line, type your city, state, and zip code. On the final line, type your telephone number. Does all of this information fit easily into four lines? If not, you might want to try a slightly smaller point size (or a different font) until it does.
4. Insert several extra lines (paragraph breaks) or press Enter at the end of the text block. Copy the text block and then insert it below the original text block. Insert a column break so that the cursor moves to the top of the right column. Copy both text blocks from the left column into the right column so that you have four text blocks, as shown. Save your document. Check the print preview to make sure that the placement of your text is correct, and then adjust and resave if necessary. If you are using clear transfer film, choose a reverse (mirror-image) orientation (see "Reversing Text" on page 19).
5. If you're using printable fabric, place it in the printer so that the printing will appear

on the fabric side. If you're using iron-on transfer film, make sure that the film side will receive the printing.

6. Print your labels. Allow the ink to dry and then cut the labels apart. Refer to "Printable Fabric" on pages 22–23 to wash the printer fabric or to "Iron-on Transfer Film" on page 20 to iron your transfers onto fabric. Hand stitch your labels to the backs of your quilts.

CARE LABELS

THE FIRST question a nonquilter usually asks me is, "How long does it take you to make a quilt?" The second is almost always, "How do I wash my quilt?" In the past, when I gave quilts as gifts I enclosed washing instructions with the gift card. The instructions usually got lost, however, and I'd eventually receive a phone call from the owner when the time came to wash the quilt. Now, I like to print a care label onto a piece of printable fabric, turn under the edges, and then sew the care label to the quilt backing along with the label bearing my name as quiltmaker.

In this section you will find examples of washing-instruction labels for hand-pieced and hand-quilted quilts, for machine-pieced and machine-quilted quilts, and for baby quilts. Use the instructions as guidelines for creating customized care labels of your own.

Washing Instructions for Hand-Pieced and Hand-Quilted Quilts

Your quilt was hand pieced and hand quilted. It should also be hand washed. Washing, no matter how carefully done, contributes to the deterioration and fading of your quilt. Therefore, it is best to wash it as infrequently as possible, spot-cleaning it with a damp cloth between washings as needed.

1. Run 6" to 8" of warm water in a bathtub. Dissolve a small amount of mild detergent (not soap) in the water before adding the quilt.
2. Press the quilt gently into the water until all parts are thoroughly wet. Gently knead the quilt and then let it soak for 20 minutes to 1 hour.
3. Drain the tub and add fresh water to rinse the quilt. Continue draining water and rinsing the quilt until the water runs clear. When you drain the tub a final time, gently press on the quilt to remove excess water.
4. Place thick towels on the quilt and press again to remove as much water as possible.
5. To lessen the strain on the quilt, use both hands to gently remove it from the tub. For a large quilt, two people might be needed for this step.
6. Spread a clean sheet or some towels in a warm, dry location. Carefully spread the quilt over the sheet or towels, gently straightening the edges and patting out wrinkles. If you're drying your quilt outdoors, cover the quilt with another clean sheet to prevent sun damage. You may have to turn the quilt over several times to dry it thoroughly. Do not fold or store the quilt until it is completely dry.

Washing Instructions for Machine-Pieced and Machine-Quilted Quilts

Washing, no matter how carefully done, contributes to the deterioration and fading of your quilt. Therefore, it is best to wash it as infrequently as possible, spot-cleaning it with a damp cloth between washings as needed.

1. Set the washing machine on the gentle or delicate cycle, at the highest water level and for the shortest cycle.
2. Dissolve a small amount of mild detergent (not soap) in the water before adding the quilt.
3. Agitate the quilt for 2 to 3 minutes; then stop the machine and soak the quilt for 20 minutes to 1 hour.
4. Restart the washing machine and finish the cycle.
5. Spread out a clean sheet or some towels in a warm, dry location. Carefully spread the quilt over the sheet or towels, gently straightening the edges and patting out wrinkles. If you're drying your quilt outdoors, cover the quilt with another clean sheet to prevent sun damage. You may have to turn the quilt over several times to dry it thoroughly. Do not fold or store the quilt until it is completely dry.

Washing Instructions for Baby Quilts

Baby quilts are usually made of sturdy cotton fabric, pieced by machine, and densely machine quilted for long use. Washing, no matter how carefully done, contributes to the deterioration and fading of your quilt. Therefore, it is best to wash it as infrequently as possible, spot-cleaning it with a damp cloth between washings as needed.

1. Set the washing machine on the gentle or delicate cycle, at the highest water level and for the shortest cycle.
2. Dissolve a small amount of mild detergent (not soap) in the water before adding the quilt. You may need to include a bath towel to balance the load.
3. If you spread it out flat to dry on a cotton sheet, your quilt will last longer than if you put it in a dryer.

Instructions for Use
Wrap one child in quilt. Squeeze gently.

Incorporating Appliqué Motifs

The following hand- and machine-appliqué techniques offer a variety of ways to embellish labels.

FUSIBLE BRODERIE PERSE

You can appliqué a beautiful border of flowers around a label by using a floral fabric from the quilt front or another floral fabric that coordinates with the quilt. Fusible appliqué is ideal for motifs with intricate edges.

Even though it may leave a few "whiskers" at the edges of the fabric, I like to use a very lightweight fusible web to keep the fused pieces soft and flexible. If you don't mind a stiffer label, you could use a medium- to heavy-weight fusible web to avoid stray threads at the edges.

Dimensions: 8" x 5½"
A floral fabric used on the front of the quilt was used to frame this broderie perse label.

Materials

- Light fabric for label background, 4" longer and 4" wider than the area to be lettered
- Scraps of floral fabrics
- Paper-backed fusible web
- Threads to match the label background and quilt backing

Making the Label

Follow these steps to appliqué a heart-shaped frame.

1. Compose your label and apply it to the middle of the light fabric, referring to the lettering instructions on pages 15–23 as needed.
2. Cut out flowers and groups of flowers from floral fabric scraps, leaving ½" margins around each piece. Place the motifs roughly in position around the lettering.
3. Following the manufacturer's instructions, apply fusible web to the wrong sides of the flowers. Some fusible web products iron on, while others are self-adhesive. If using the iron-on web, be careful not to touch the fusible adhesive to your iron.

Flowers for Appliqu

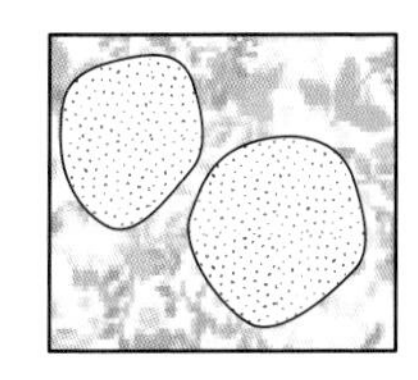

Fuse web to wrong side of fabric.

4. Cut out the flowers from the fused fabric, keeping the paper backing attached and taking care to cut exactly along the edge of each design. No seam allowances are required.

5. Remove the paper backing and position the flowers around the label in a pleasing frame, overlapping the edges as desired.

6. Following the manufacturer's instructions for your fusible web, press the inner edges of the floral frame to secure the pieces. Leave the outer edges free so that you can trim the label fabric later.
7. Referring to "Invisible Machine Appliqué" on page 33 and using bobbin thread that matches the label fabric, stitch the inner edges of the flowers and any overlapped edges onto the label. Trim the excess label fabric underneath the floral frame, leaving a ¼" seam allowance outside the stitched lines.
8. Before you layer the quilt sandwich, position the label on the quilt backing and press it in place. Using bobbin thread that matches the quilt backing, machine appliqué the outer edges of the floral frame onto the backing. Carefully cut away the quilt backing under the label area, leaving a ¼" seam allowance.

Trim, leaving a ¼" seam allowance.

NEEDLE-TURN APPLIQUÉ

BASICALLY, TRADITIONAL needle-turn appliqué happens in two steps. The first step is to turn under and stabilize the raw edge of the fabric, and the second step is to stitch the fold of the appliqué shape in place. For needle-turn appliqué you'll want to use a Sharp needle, which is longer and thinner than a quilting needle, enabling you to take finer stitches.

Materials

- Appliqué motif(s)
- Threads to match the label background and/or quilt backing
- Size 10 or 11 Sharp needle

Making the Label

Follow these steps to use needle-turn appliqué in a label.

1. Including a scant ¼" seam allowance, cut out each shape you want to appliqué onto your label. Clip the seam allowance along inner curves and at inner corners.

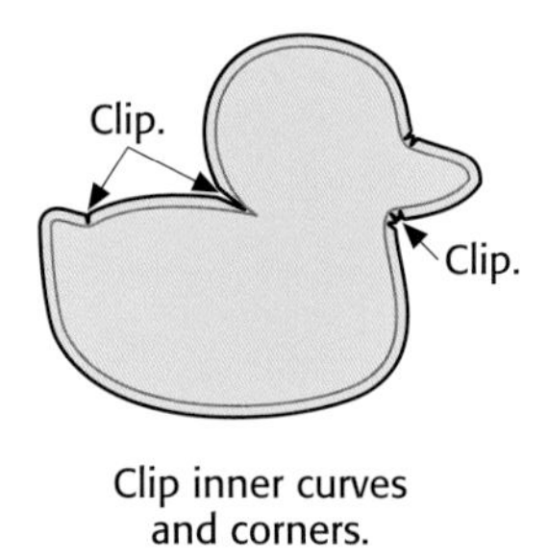

Clip inner curves and corners.

2. Pin or baste the shapes in position on your label fabric.
3. Thread a size 10 or 11 Sharp needle with an 18" length of thread, and tie a knot at one end of the thread.

4. Turn under the edge of an appliqué shape. Bring the needle up through both the background fabric and the folded edge of the appliqué shape. Move the needle straight off the appliqué shape and insert it into the background fabric at that point. Move the needle underneath the background fabric, parallel to the edge of the appliqué shape, and bring it back up about ⅛" away, catching only two or three threads of the appliqué shape. (If you're right-handed, stitch from right to left. If you're left-handed, stitch from left to right.)

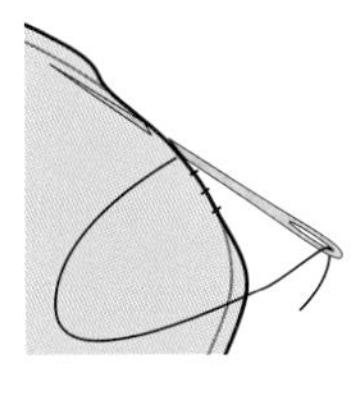

5. Continue taking stitches as described in step 4, keeping the stitch length consistent as you go. To end a line of appliqué stitches, take the needle to the wrong side of your work. Make two small stitches inside your stitched line, making small knots by bringing the needle through each loop you create as you take the stitch. Clip the thread.

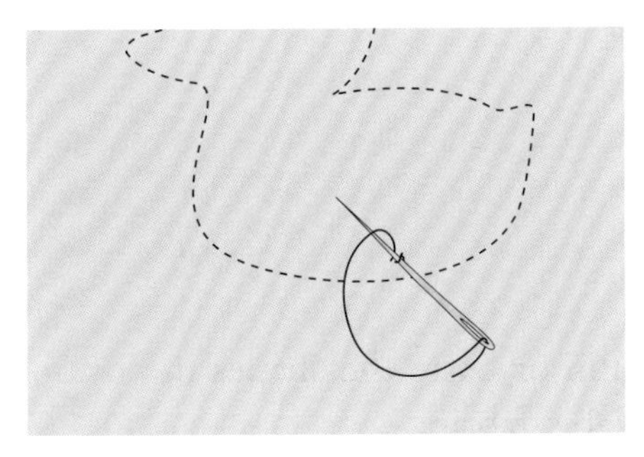

FREEZER-PAPER APPLIQUÉ

Backing motifs with freezer paper is a secure way to prepare the appliqué pieces before stitching them to a label with hidden or decorative stitches.

Materials

- Floral fabric
- Tracing paper
- Black permanent marker
- White fabric or paper to use as tracing background
- Masking tape
- Freezer paper
- Scissors for cutting paper
- Water-soluble glue stick
- Spray bottle filled with water

Making the Label

Follow these steps to use freezer-paper appliqué in a label.

1. Place tracing paper over the right side of the floral fabric. Using the permanent marker, trace the motif you'd like to appliqué. If you plan to use more than one motif from a single piece of fabric, make sure to keep at least ¾" between each to allow for seam allowances. At a corner of the tracing paper, write the word "front."

2. Turn the tracing paper over so that the word "front" is reversed, and tape it onto the white fabric or paper. Tape a piece of freezer paper on top of your tracing, with the dull, *unwaxed* side facing up. For each

motif you plan to use, trace the reversed shape onto the unwaxed side of the freezer paper and then cut out the shape exactly on the outline.

3. Place the waxed side of the freezer-paper template against the wrong side of the floral fabric, carefully matching the template shape to the fabric design. Press the template to the fabric using a hot, dry iron.

4. Cut out the shape, leaving a ¼" seam allowance beyond the edges of the freezer paper. Clip any inner curves or corners, and trim outer corners to 3/16".

5. Apply water-soluble glue stick to the wrong side of the seam allowances. Fold the seam allowances onto the freezer paper.

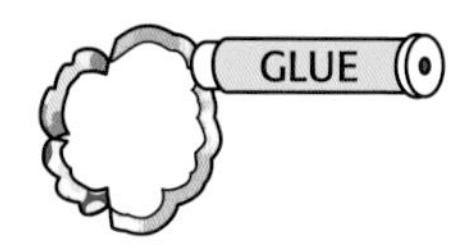

6. Position each prepared appliqué design on your label and stitch it in place, referring to "Needle-Turn Appliqué" on page 30 or "Invisible Machine Appliqué" on page 33.

7. Trim away the fabric behind each appliqué, leaving a ¼" seam allowance inside your stitched lines.

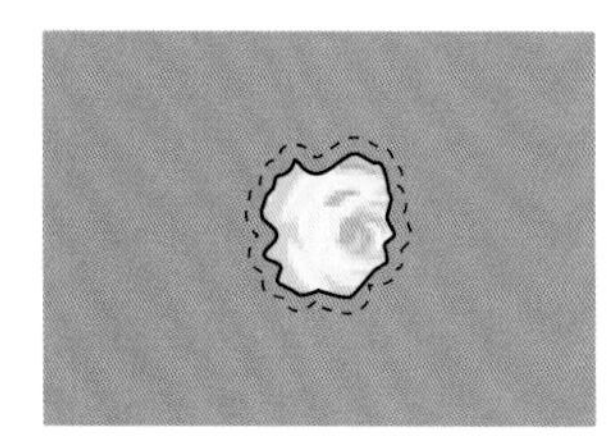

8. Spray the label with water to dissolve the glue residue. Remove the freezer paper and press the completed label.

REVERSE APPLIQUÉ

With reverse appliqué, an opening is cut in the backing fabric that allows the label fabric underneath to show through. The shape of the opening can be a circle, a heart, or anything you like.

Dimensions: 6" x 6"

I reverse appliquéd this label to a quilt backing where there was an open space in the fabric design. To better frame the label I appliquéd extra flowers around the edges, using freezer-paper appliqué.

Materials

- Lettered label
- Quilt backing
- Erasable fabric pen or pencil
- Black permanent marker
- Freezer paper
- Scissors for cutting paper

Making the Label

Follow these steps to use reverse appliqué in a label.

1. Using the erasable fabric pen or pencil, mark the outline of the desired opening on the lettered label. Using the black permanent marker, trace that shape onto the uncoated side of freezer paper and cut out the shape on the marked lines.
2. Place the shiny side of the freezer-paper template against the right side of the backing fabric, where you want to place the label. Using a hot, dry iron, press the template to the fabric. Mark around the template with the erasable pen or pencil. Remove the freezer paper and cut away the backing ¼" inside the marked lines.
3. Position your label underneath the opening in the backing fabric and pin it in place. Turn under the edges of the opening by ¼", pinning or thread-basting the turned edge in place. Clip any inner curves and angles, if necessary, to make the seam allowances turn under smoothly.

4. Appliqué the edges to the label fabric with hidden or decorative stitches. Refer to "Needle-Turn Appliqué" on page 30 or "Invisible Machine Appliqué" above right for stitching instructions.
5. On the wrong side of the work, trim away the label fabric ¼" outside your stitching line. Press the completed label.

INVISIBLE MACHINE APPLIQUÉ

MACHINE APPLIQUÉ is my preferred method, because I get nice results in a short time. Both fusible and freezer-paper techniques are well suited to invisible machine appliqué. Decrease the top tension on your sewing machine and use transparent thread on top. If your machine allows, increase the bobbin-case tension by a quarter turn, and use fine machine-embroidery thread in the bobbin. Stitch with a size 70 machine needle and an open-toe appliqué foot.

DIMENSIONS: 8½" x 7"
I applied these flowers with lightweight fusible web and finished the edges with invisible machine appliqué.

Materials

- Lettered label
- Fabric motifs prepared for appliqué. (See "Fusible Broderie Perse" on page 29 for fusible-web methods or "Freezer-Paper Appliqué" on page 31 for freezer-paper techniques.)
- Sewing machine with blind hemstitch capability
- Transparent thread for needle
- Machine-embroidery thread for bobbin

Making the Label

Follow these steps to use invisible machine appliqué in a label.

1. Set your sewing machine for a short, blind hemstitch. The machine will take four to seven straight stitches and then swing left to take one wider stitch. Position the needle so it just touches the outer edge of the appliqué. Then adjust the stitch width so that the needle catches just two or three threads when it swings left. Adjust the stitch length so that the straight stitching runs for about ⅛" between the wide swings of the needle. Practice making adjustments until you like the look of your blind hemstitching, and take notes for future reference. I keep my favorite settings taped to my machine so that I can see at a glance what works best for me.

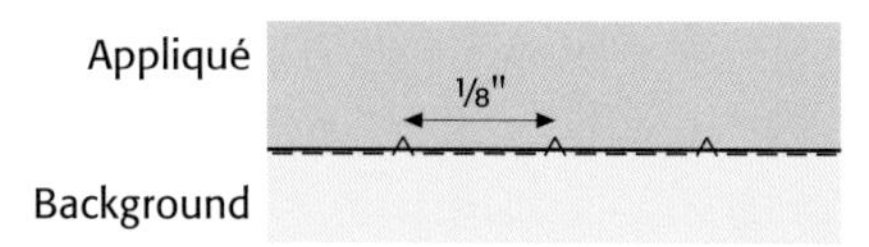

2. Position the prepared appliqué pieces on your label fabric, starting with the bottom pieces. You will stitch those first and then build up from there.
3. Position the needle in the label fabric so that it just touches the edge of the first appliqué shape. Blind hemstitch around the shape. The straight stitches will be made in the ditch and the sideways swing of the needle will just catch the edge of the appliqué shape.
4. To end, simply stop stitching, clip the threads, and pull the thread tail to the wrong side of the label. Clip the threads to ½" long.

STRAIGHT-STITCH APPLIQUÉ

You may know this technique as topstitching. It's very strong and durable—a plus for baby and children's quilts. It works best for straight edges and gentle curves.

Materials

- Fabrics for appliqué
- Lettered label
- Quilt backing
- Pins or thread for basting appliqués
- Thread for topstitching

Making the Label

Follow these steps to use straight-stitch appliqué in a label.

1. Prepare your appliqué pieces by turning under the edges. Press or baste the turned-under edges to hold them in place.
2. Pin the label to the backing fabric. Position the appliqué shapes on the label fabric and pin or thread-baste them in place. Using your sewing machine, straight stitch very close to the edge of each appliqué shape.

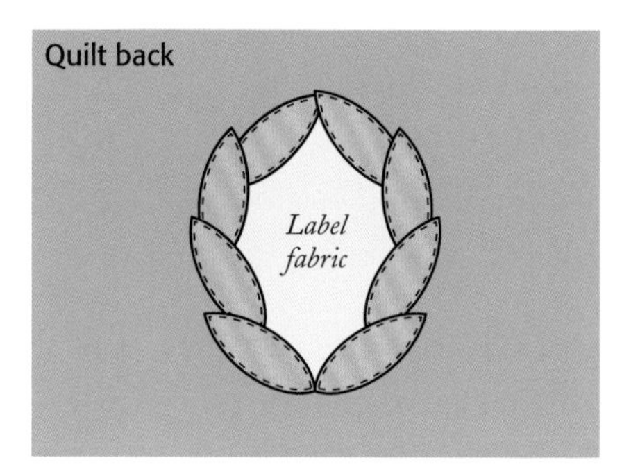

3. To end the stitching, take a few backstitches and stop. Clip the threads, pull them to the wrong side of the label, and clip them to ½". Remove any basting threads.

Setting a Label into a Quilt Block

WHAT BETTER WAY to display a label than to set it in the same block used on the front of the quilt? Explore the following methods for surrounding a label with patchwork.

LOG CABIN BLOCK

DIMENSIONS: 9" x 9" Finished block

We finally made a label for my daughter Elaine's first quilt. For the label, we weren't able to match the dark fabrics to the ones used in the quilt top, but we found new ones in similar colors.

Materials

- 1 square of medium-value fabric for center of block*
- 1½" strips of 3 different dark fabrics
- 1½" strips of 1 light fabric
- 6 squares, 1½" x 1½", of accent fabric

*The lettering shown in the photo was printed on a computer and fits in a 3" x 3" space. The cut size of the square was 3½" x 3½". If your message is too large for an area of this size, enlarge the center square as desired, referring to "Enlarging Patterns" on page 18.

Making the Label

Follow these steps to make a label from a Log Cabin block.

1. Compose your label and letter it on the medium-value square, referring to the lettering instructions on pages 15–23 as needed. Leave a ¼" seam allowance around the edges of the lettered square.
2. Sew a 1½" dark strip to the right-hand edge of the lettered square. Press the seam allowance toward the dark fabric. Trim the strip even with the edge of the label. Sew another strip of the same dark fabric to the bottom of the label. Press the seam allowance toward the dark fabric and trim the strip even with the edge of the label.

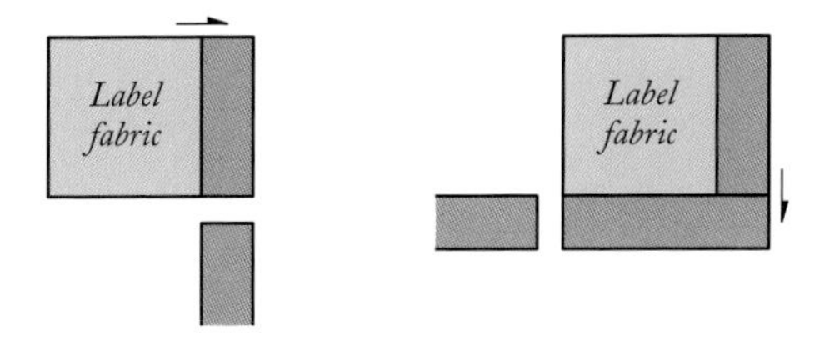

3. Sew a 1½" accent square to the end of a 1½" light strip. Press the seam allowance toward the light fabric. Sew this strip to the left edge of the label, placing the accent square alongside the second dark strip and aligning the seams. Press the seam allowance toward the light fabric. Trim the strip even with the edge of the label.

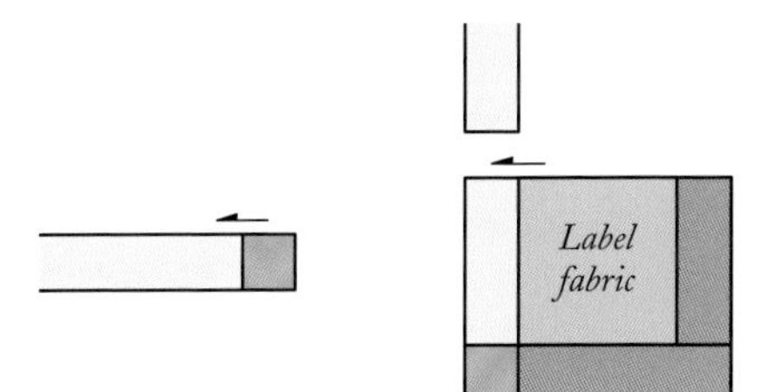

4. Sew another 1½" accent square to the end of a 1½" light strip. Press the seam allowance toward the light fabric. Sew this strip to the top of the label, placing the accent strip alongside the dark fabric. Press the seam allowance toward the light fabric and trim the end of the strip even with the edge of the label.

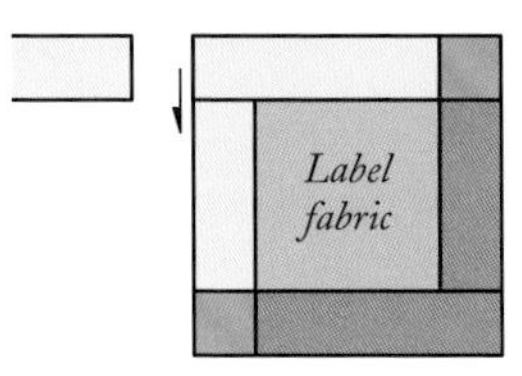

5. Sew two more rounds of dark strips and light strips with accent squares to the block. Press the completed Log Cabin block.

6. Turn under a ¼" seam allowance on each side of the Log Cabin block and hand or machine stitch it to the quilt backing.

KALEIDOSCOPE BLOCK

Kaleidoscope blocks make striking quilt labels. Refer to the instructions below to stitch up one of your own.

Materials

- 4" x 4" square of light fabric for center of block*
- ½ yard of kaleidoscope fabric for triangles**
- ½ yard of fabric for background
- Freezer paper
- Medium-point permanent marker

*The lettering shown in the photo was printed on a computer and fits in a 3" x 3" space. If your message is too large for an area of this size, enlarge the block pattern as desired, referring to "Enlarging Patterns" on page 18.

**This yardage is for triangles that are not fussy cut. If you want to fussy cut your triangles, allow additional fabric for eight repeats. The yardage required will vary depending on the fabric design. Cut eight rectangles 6¼" wide and the length of the pattern repeat. Layer the repeating motifs and position pins through common points in each layer. Smooth and pin the layers together. Cut through the layers to make a set of eight identical triangles for use in the Kaleidoscope block. Pin the set together until ready to use.

Dimensions: 13" x 13"
Fussy cutting Kaleidoscope blocks takes a great deal of fabric, and you end up with lots of leftover pieces in matched stacks. I used leftovers from a quilt top to make this label.

Cutting

From the kaleidoscope fabric, cut:

- 4 squares, 6¼" x 6¼"; cut each square in half diagonally to make a total of 8 triangles

From the background fabric, cut:

- 2 squares, 6¼" x 6¼"; cut each square in half diagonally to make a total of 4 triangles
- 4 rectangles, 2¾" x 8½"

Making the Label

Follow these steps to make a label from a Kaleidoscope block.

1. Using the permanent marker, trace the trimming template pattern from page 38 onto freezer paper and cut it out on the marked lines.
2. Stack the background rectangles right sides up and place the template on top. Using a rotary cutter and ruler, trim the ends of the rectangles even with the template.
3. Pair four kaleidoscope and background triangles with right sides together. Using a ¼" seam allowance, stitch the pairs together as shown. Press the seam allowances toward the kaleidoscope fabric.

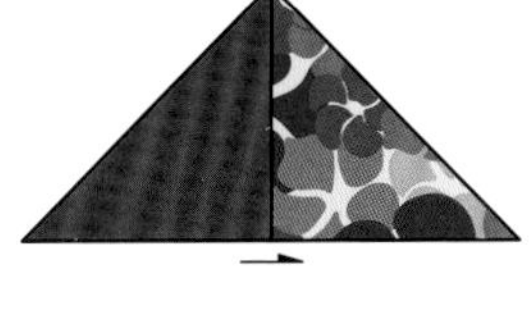

4. With right sides together, place the angled background pieces on top of the four remaining triangles. Sew a ¼" seam along the edge of each pair as shown. Press the seam allowances toward the kaleidoscope fabric.

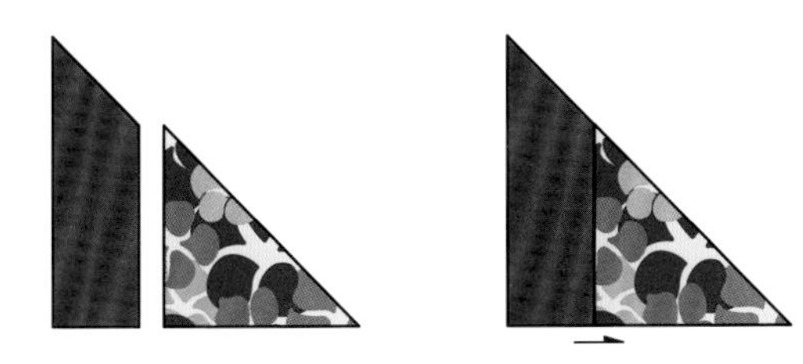

5. Layer a unit from step 3 with one from step 4, right sides together, and stitch along the long edge. Press the seam allowance open. This completes a quarter-block. Repeat for the remaining three pairs.

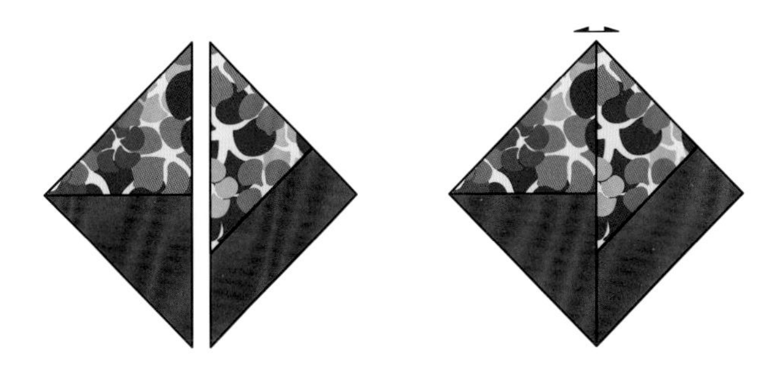

6. Layer two quarter-blocks with right sides together, so that the background fabrics meet. Stitch from the center (kaleidoscope fabric) to the outer edge (template piece). Press the seam allowance open. Repeat for the remaining two quarter-block units.

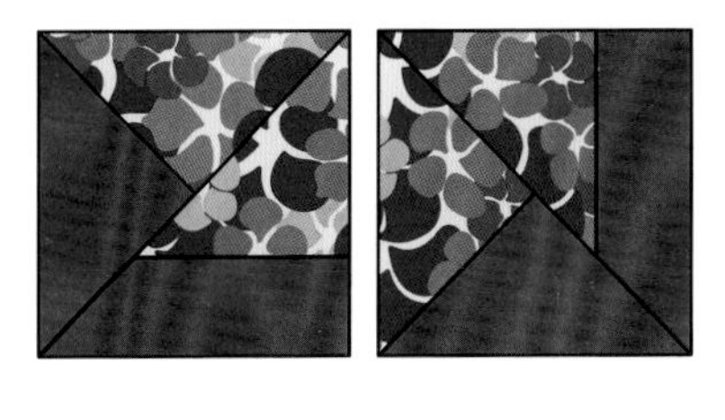

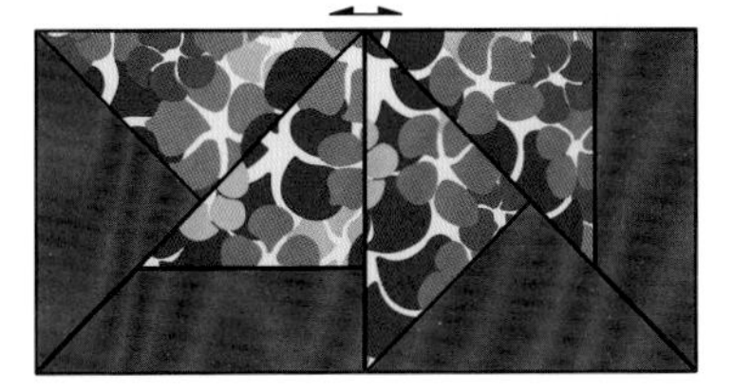

7. Stitch the two units together, carefully matching the center seams. Press the seam allowance open.

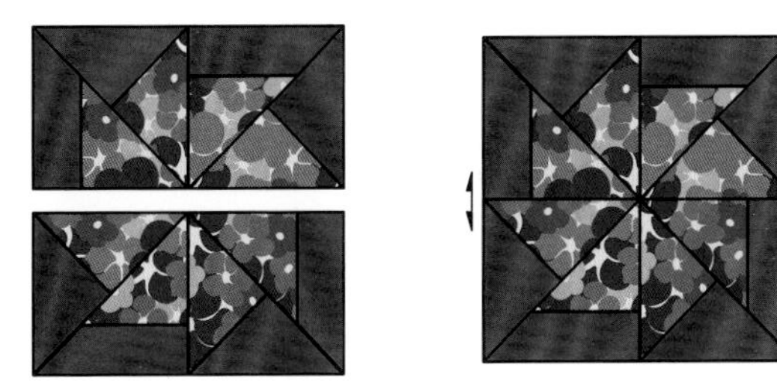

8. Compose and letter your label, using the square of light fabric and referring to the lettering instructions on pages 15–23 as needed.
9. Trace the label center pattern below onto the uncoated side of freezer paper and cut it out on the marked lines. Press the shiny side of the template to the wrong side of your lettered fabric, making sure that the lettering on your label is straight and centered within the template shape. Cut around the freezer paper, leaving a ¼" seam allowance beyond the template edge.
10. Turn under a ¼" seam allowance on each edge of the label center and appliqué it to the center of the Kaleidoscope block, matching the points on the label center to the seams of the block. Turn under the edges of the block and attach the label to the quilt backing.

Triangle seam line

Trimming Template
Cut 1 from freezer paper.

Label Center
Cut 1 from lettered fabric.

INTERLOCKING SQUARES

FOLLOW THESE steps to create a paper-pieced Interlocking Squares block with a label at the center.

DIMENSIONS: 6" x 6"
Strong complementary colors add zing to this label.

Materials

- 3½" x 3½" square of light fabric for label*
- 2¼" x 20" turquoise strip for interlocking square
- 2¾" x 20" red-orange strip for interlocking square
- 2" x 40" strip of black-and-green print for background (pieces 15, 16, 18, 19, 21, 22, 24, and 25)
- Tracing paper
- Marking pen or pencil
- Ruler
- Air-soluble marker

*The lettering shown in the photo was printed on a computer and fits in a 3" x 3" space. If your message is too large for an area of this size, enlarge the block pattern as desired, referring to "Enlarging Patterns" on page 18.

Making the Label

Follow these steps to make a label set in an Interlocking Squares block.

1. From the turquoise strip, cut two squares, 2¼" x 2¼", for pieces 14, 17, 20, and 23. Set aside the remaining fabric for pieces 2, 4, 6, and 8.
2. From the red-orange strip, cut two squares, 2¾" x 2¾", for pieces 10, 11, 12, and 13. Set aside the remaining fabric for pieces 3, 5, 7, and 9.
3. Compose and letter your label, using the square of light fabric and referring to the lettering instructions on pages 15–23 as needed.
4. Trace the block pattern from page 41 onto tracing paper, including the numbers.
5. On the wrong side of the traced pattern, place the lettered square on top of piece 1, with the right side of the fabric facing up. Make sure that the lettering is straight and square with the block edges and that at least ¼" of the fabric extends beyond the seam lines on all sides. You can check the positioning by holding the paper up to a light or by using a light box.
6. With the right side *down*, position the remaining turquoise strip for piece 2, matching raw edges and overlapping the seam line between pieces 1 and 2. Do not trim away any excess fabric from the strip. Pin the fabric for piece 2 in place or hold it in position by dabbing the fabric with a glue stick.
7. Set your machine to 10 to 12 stitches per inch. Turn the foundation to the marked side so that the fabric is underneath the paper, and sew along the solid line between pieces 1 and 2. (Do not sew into the dotted line. This is a partial seam and will be finished later.) Remove the piece from the sewing

machine, open the fabrics, and finger-press the partial seam. Double-check to make sure that at least ¼" of fabric extends beyond the seam lines on all sides of piece 2.

8. In the same manner and working clockwise, position piece 3 and sew on the line that borders pieces 1 and 2, stitching along the entire line. Remove the piece from the machine and check to make sure that at least ¼" of fabric extends beyond the seam lines. Trim the seam allowance to ¼" and finger-press it open. Work your way around the center, alternating colors until you are back at the beginning. When attaching piece 9, fold the dangling strip of piece 2 out of the way. Finally, sew the partial seam along the dotted line; then open the pieces and finger-press the seam. Press.

9. Cut the 2¾" red-orange squares once on the diagonal to make four triangles. Sew the triangles (pieces 10, 11, 12, and 13) to the center unit. Trim the seam allowances to ¼" and finger-press.

10. The outer corner units are made separately and then sewn to the paper-pieced unit. Cut the 2¼" turquoise squares in half on the diagonal to make four triangles (pieces 14, 17, 20, and 23).

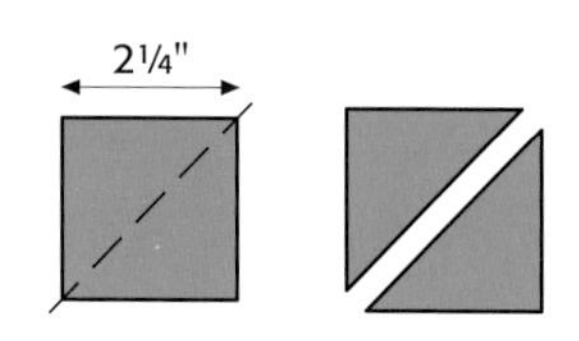

11. Sew these four triangles to the 2" strip of background fabric, aligning one short edge of each triangle with the edge of the strip and leaving 2" between the triangles as shown above right. Cut the strip between the triangles as shown. Press toward the background fabric.

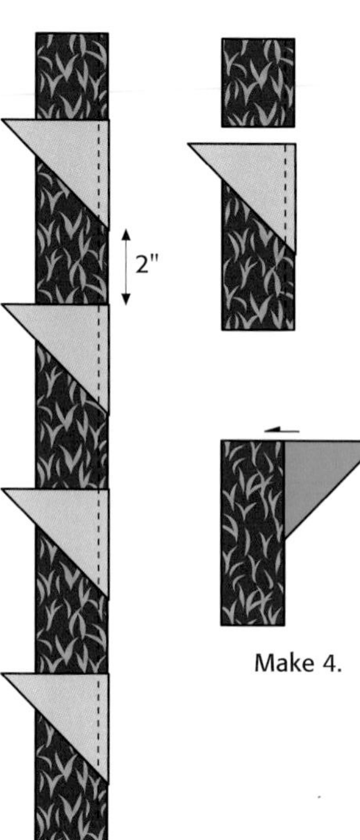

Make 4.

12. For pieces 16, 19, 22, and 25, sew a 2" strip of background fabric across the top of each triangle unit, as shown. Trim the strip 2" beyond the end of each triangle. These corner units are oversized. On the foundation pattern, piece 14 is marked with points A, B, and C. If you didn't enlarge the pattern, the distance between these points is 1". (If you enlarged the pattern, measure between points A and B to determine the distance.) Measure this distance on the corner units you just pieced, to locate points A and C. Mark these points with an air-soluble marker.

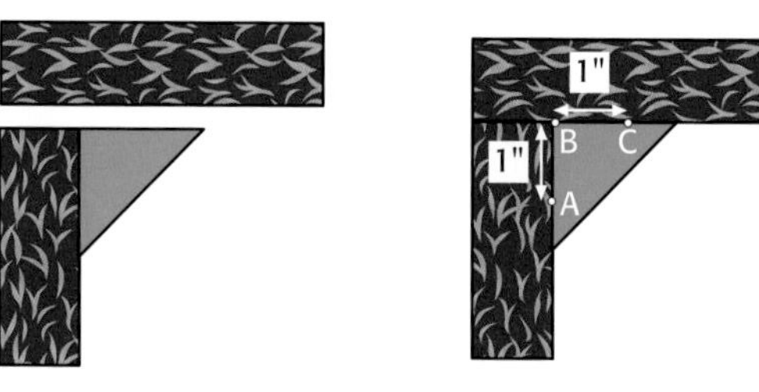

Make 4.

13. Pin the corner units to the block with right sides together, matching points A and C with the seam intersections on the block. Sew the pieces together. Trim the seam allowances and finger-press them open. Turn under the edges of the block and attach the label to the quilt backing.

Completed Block

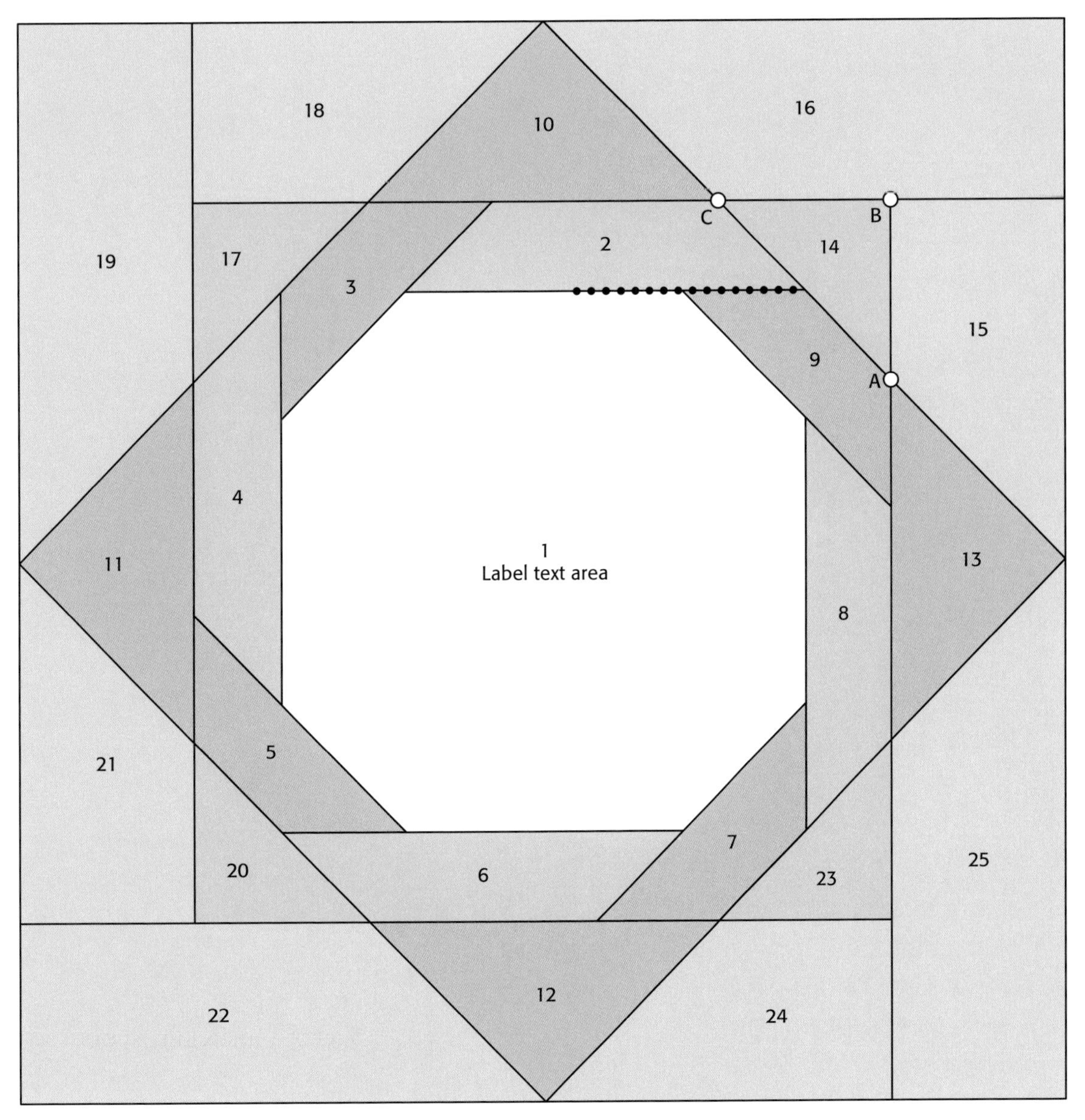

Interlocking Squares Paper-Piecing Pattern

EIGHTEEN-POINT STAR BLOCK

WITH THE text in a center circle, multiple-point Star or Pinwheel blocks make dynamic quilt labels.

DIMENSIONS: 12" DIAMETER
LABEL DIMENSIONS: 5" DIAMETER

I first made this label for a wedding quilt and then re-created it for this book. All the best labels walk out the door! On the front of the original quilt, the striped fabric was used as a border.

Materials

Yardage is based on 42"-wide fabric unless otherwise noted.

- 6" x 6" square of light fabric for label*
- ¼ yard of fabric for star points
- ¼ yard of fabric for background
- Freezer paper
- Black permanent marker
- Scissors or dull rotary blade for cutting freezer paper
- Rotary cutter, acrylic ruler, and cutting mat
- Straight pins

*The lettering shown in the photo was printed on a computer and fits in a 5" diameter. If your message is too large for an area of this size, enlarge the block pattern as desired, referring to "Enlarging Patterns" on page 18.

Making the Label

Follow these steps to make a label from an Eighteen-Point Star block.

1. Compose and letter your label, using the square of light fabric and referring to the lettering instructions on pages 15–23 as needed. Make sure to keep the lettering within the boundaries of the circle pattern on page 44.
2. Trace the circle pattern and three copies of the A-B star pattern from page 44 onto the uncoated side of freezer paper. Cut out the circle on the marked line. Cut out the A-B pattern as one piece, about ½" from the marked lines.

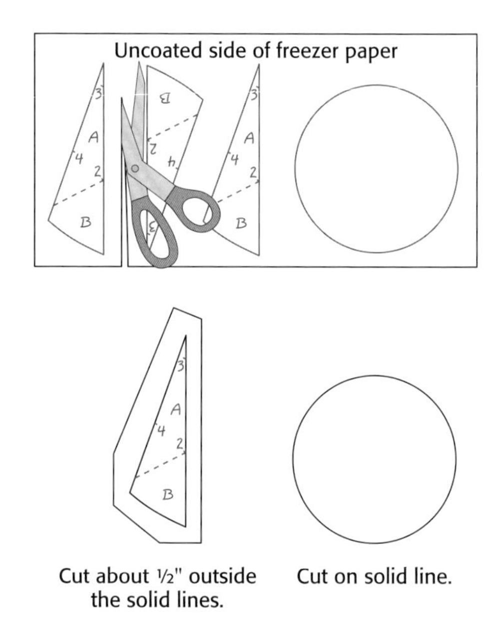

3. Cut fifteen 2½" x 6¼" rectangles from freezer paper. Divide the rectangles into three stacks of five, with the shiny sides facing down. Pin an A-B template to the top of each stack, with the markings facing up, and pin each stack together with straight pins.
4. Unthread your sewing machine and stitch over the lines of an A-B template, including the dotted line between sections A and B. Working from the edge of the piece

inward, make a few stitches to indicate marks 3 and 4.

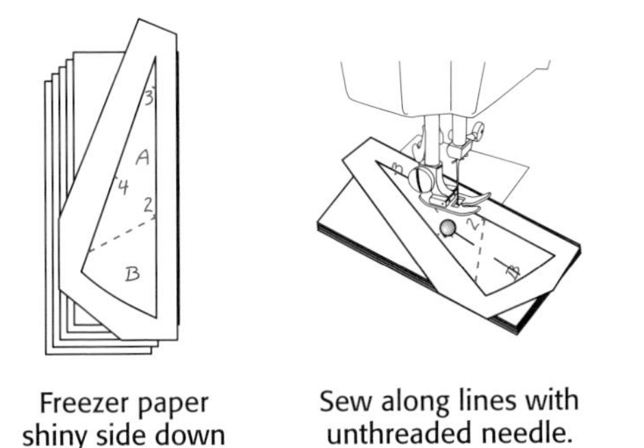

Freezer paper shiny side down

Sew along lines with unthreaded needle.

5. Repeat step 4 for the remaining stacks of freezer-paper rectangles. Cut along the outer edges of each A-B pattern piece, on the perforated lines. Do *not* cut on the line between sections A and B.

6. Fold each freezer-paper piece, with uncoated sides together, along the perforated line between sections A and B. Position the pattern pieces on the wrong side of your star fabric, with the shiny sides facing down, leaving at least ½" between the pieces to allow for seam allowances. Press section A of each template to the star fabric. If you are using a striped fabric in piece A, take care to orient the stripes on the fabric as desired. Press the freezer paper to the wrong side of the fabric with a hot, dry iron. Using a rotary cutter and an acrylic ruler, cut out the pieces exactly ¼" from the edges of section A, for seam allowances.

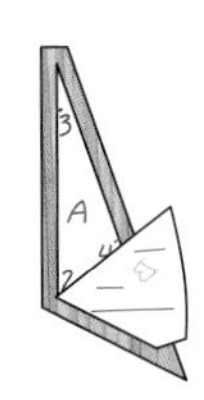

7. Cut eighteen 3" x 3" squares of background fabric.

8. Align the edges of a background square with a star piece along the A-B edge, with right sides together. Keeping the wide end of the pattern piece folded back, sew right next to the freezer-paper fold. Press the seam allowance away from the star fabric and press the B section of the pattern to the wrong side of the background square. Using a rotary cutter and ruler, cut exactly ¼" from the edges of section B. Repeat to make the remaining 17 star-point units.

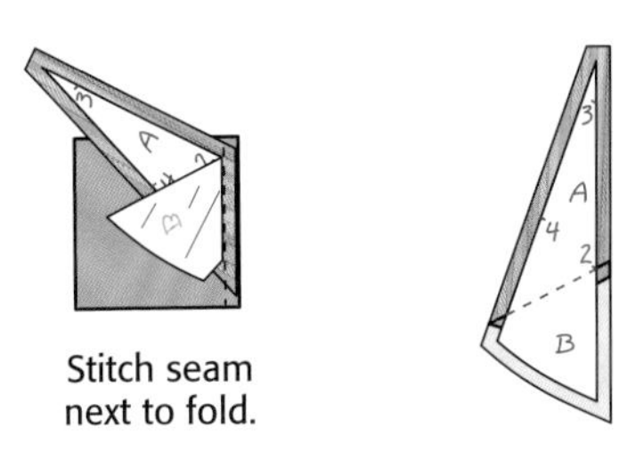

Stitch seam next to fold.

9. Sew the 18 star points together, working counterclockwise around the star and matching point 1 to mark 3 and point 2 to mark 4, until all the units have been joined. Press all the seam allowances in the same direction. Less than ¼" from the outer edge, run a machine basting or gathering stitch. Draw up the thread just enough to turn under the seam allowance at the outside edge and create a smooth circle. Press.

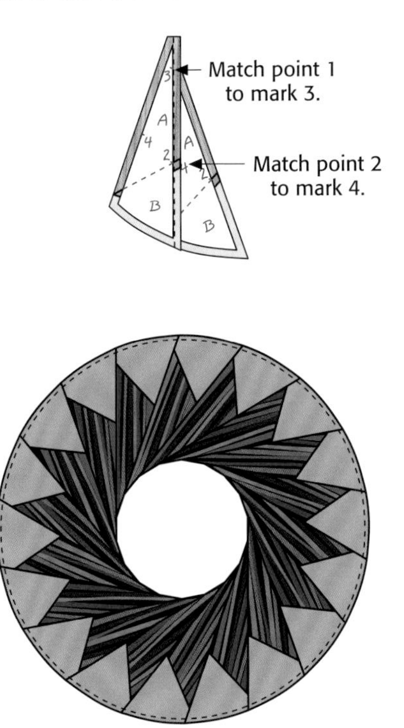

Baste a scant ¼" from outer edge.

10. Center the freezer-paper circle, shiny side down, on the wrong side of your label fabric and press it in place. Cut the circle from the fabric, leaving a ¼" seam allowance beyond the template edge. Gather, ease, and turn under the edge of the fabric circle and press it. Position the circle at the center of the star, pin, and appliqué it in place by hand or machine, referring to "Needle-Turn Appliqué" on page 30 or to "Invisible Machine Appliqué" on page 33.

11. Remove all of the freezer-paper pieces from the Star block. To attach the finished label to a quilt backing, pin and machine blindstitch it in place. Carefully cut away the quilt backing underneath the label, leaving a ¼" seam allowance beyond the template edge. Press.

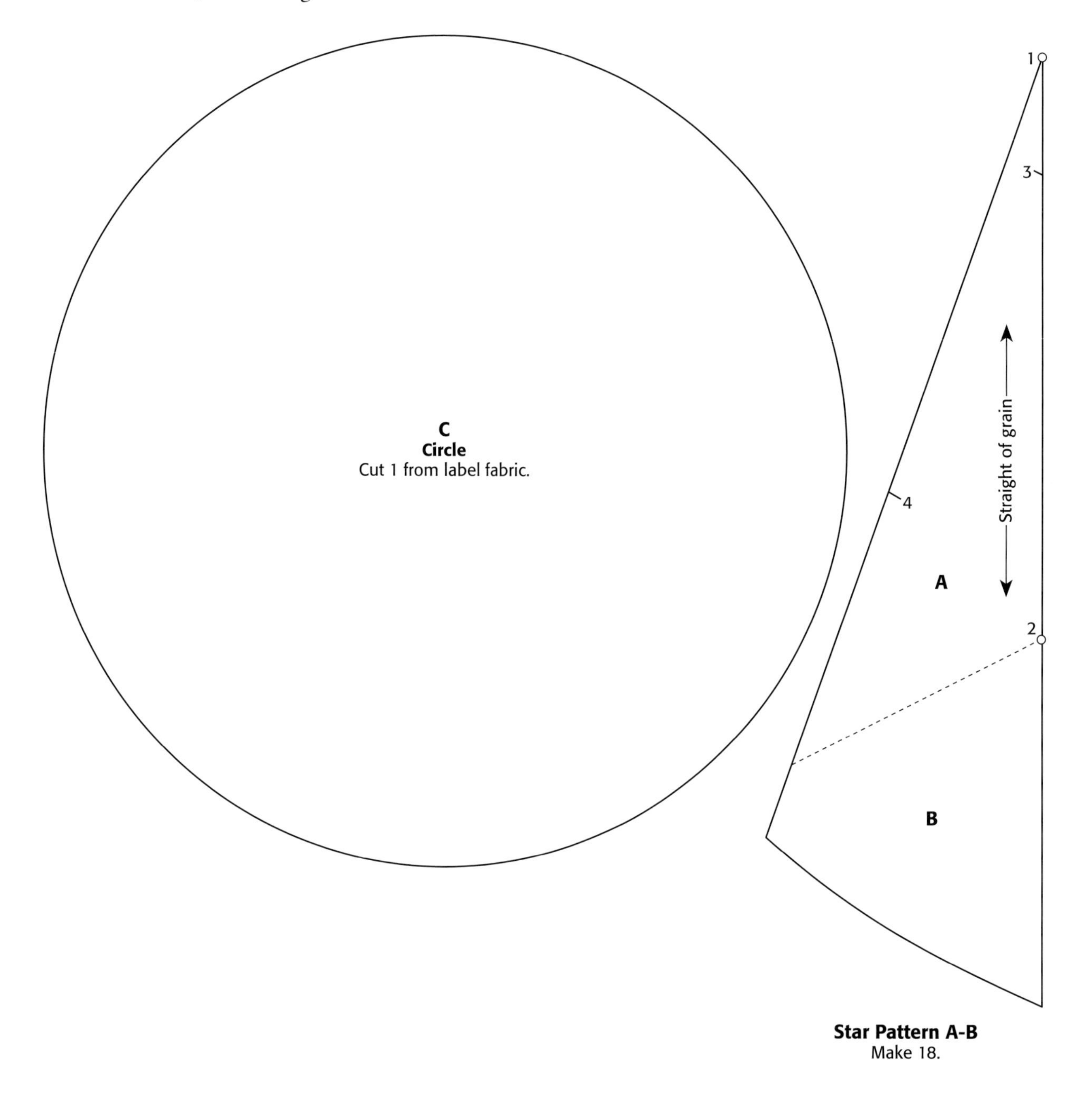

Star Pattern A-B
Make 18.

Cards and Pockets

THE FOLLOWING PROJECTS will send your creativity soaring. Make one or all, and see if you can come up with other innovative ideas for pocket labels.

FABRIC CARD WITH ENVELOPE

WHEN YOU have a lot of information to document for a quilt, a fabric card in its own envelope is a nice solution. This envelope holds a fabric card equivalent to a sheet of 8½" x 11" paper folded in quarters, which is large enough to accommodate a great deal of text.

DIMENSIONS: ENVELOPE 5½" x 4½", CARD 5¼" x 8"

For this two-part label, a fabric envelope is stitched to the back of the quilt. The label is tethered to the envelope by a ribbon. A silk-ribbon rose anchors the ribbon to the label, which can be folded and placed inside the envelope. I applied the computer-generated lettering with an iron-on transfer.

Materials

- 8½" x 11" piece of printable fabric or untreated cotton for card
- 5¼" x 8" piece of fusible interfacing
- 10" x 10" square of fabric for outer envelope
- 10" x 10" square of fabric for envelope lining
- Freezer paper
- Permanent black marker
- 12" length of narrow ribbon for tether*
- Silk-ribbon rose
- Sew-on snap or Velcro dot for envelope closure

*I attach ribbon tethers to finished card and envelope pieces. If you'd prefer to hide one or more of the ribbon ends inside a seam, insert the ribbon between pieces of fabric when you sew them together.

Making the Envelope

Follow these steps to make a fabric envelope.

1. Using the permanent marker, trace the envelope pattern from page 48 onto the uncoated side of freezer paper and cut it out on the lines. Fold the envelope fabric in half, with right sides together. Press the shiny side of the template onto the envelope fabric, aligning it with the fold. Carefully cut the double layer of envelope fabric along the edge of the freezer paper (the seam allowance has already been added to the pattern). Do not cut along the fold. Remove the freezer paper from the fabric.
2. Cut an envelope from the lining fabric as in step 1, using the same freezer-paper template. A freezer-paper template can be used several times, until it no longer adheres to fabric when ironed.

Making an Envelope Pattern

You can make an envelope pattern from any paper envelope. Open the paper envelope by moistening the glue on the side and bottom flaps; then lay the envelope flat. Trace the envelope onto freezer paper, making the side flaps a little longer so that they'll meet or overlap slightly. Press the template onto your envelope fabric and cut out the envelope, adding a ¼" seam allowance as you go. Repeat to make an envelope lining. Assemble the envelope, referring to the following instructions.

3. Unfold the envelope and lining pieces, place them right sides together, and sew around the edges, leaving a 2½" opening for turning. Clip across the corners and angles, and turn the envelope right side out. Press. Slip-stitch the opening closed.

4. Fold the side flaps in, overlapping the edges, and slip-stitch them together. Bring up the bottom flap, pin it in place, and slip-stitch the edges to the side flaps, taking care not to catch the back of the envelope or the lining in your stitching. On the top flap, sew half of a snap closure or Velcro dot to the underside of the point. Sew the other half of the closure to the bottom flap so that the closures will meet.

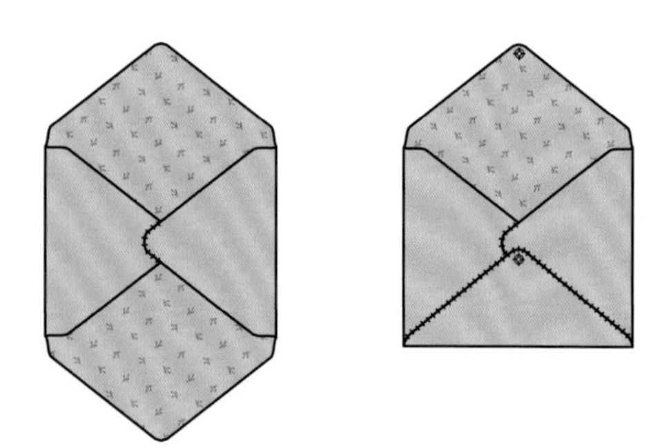

5. Position the envelope on the completed quilt back and slip-stitch it in place. Sew one end of the ribbon inside the envelope.

Making the Card

Follow these steps to make a fabric card.

1. Using the card fabric, compose and letter your label, referring to the lettering instructions on pages 15–23 as needed. You can letter just one side of the card or both, or you can make two cards from a single piece of 8½" x 11" fabric, as shown below.

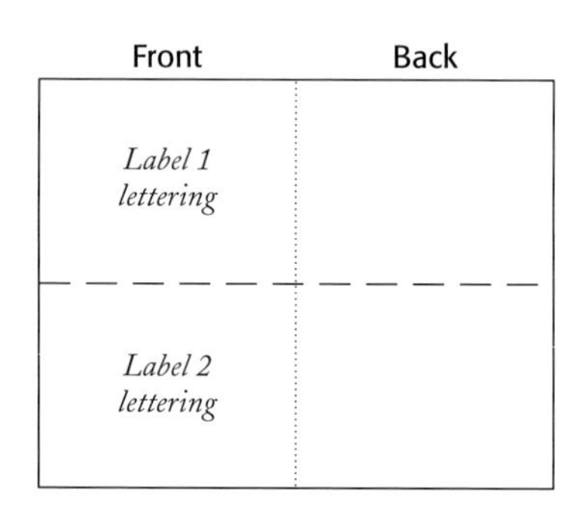

Two cards from an 8½" x 11" sheet

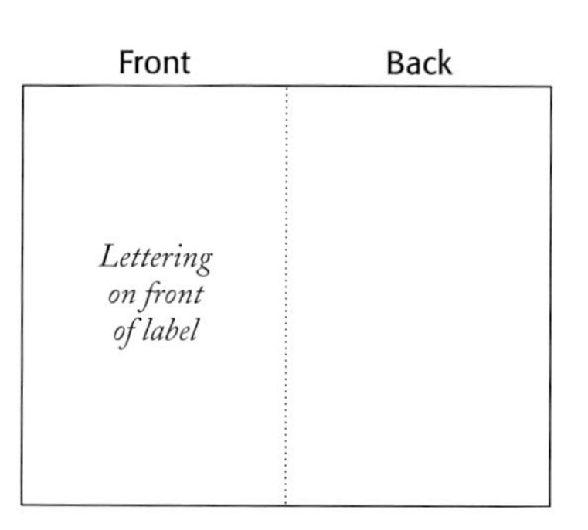

One card from an 8½" x 11" sheet

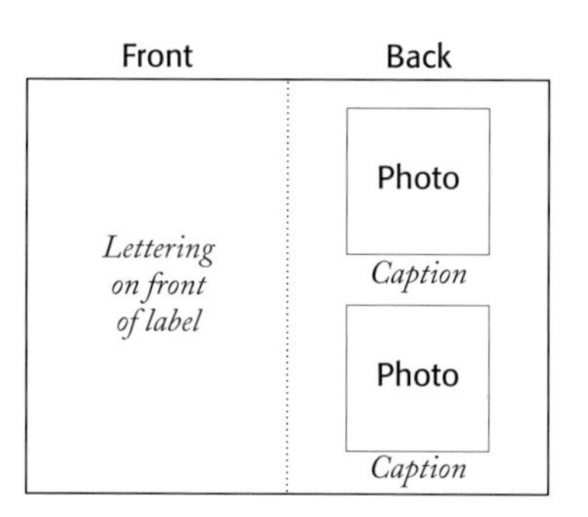

One card from an 8½" x 11" sheet, with lettering on the front and captioned photos on the back

Formatting a Two-Sided Document

If you're planning to make a computer-lettered, double-sided label, use a landscape orientation for your document. Format the page with 1" margins at the edges and a 1½" space between the two columns of text. Type the text for the front of the label; then insert a column break. Enter the text (or photos) for the back of the label into the right column. Two 3" x 3" photos with captions will fit in a column; insert a photo and then type a caption, and repeat for the second photo. Check the print preview before printing your label.

Labeling Bed Quilts

If you want to use an envelope label on a bed quilt, position the envelope near the center of the backing. It won't be noticeable when the quilt is in use on a bed.

2. Fold the card in half widthwise with the printing inside. Position the fusible interfacing on the unlettered side of the fabric so that one edge lies along the fold and the others are ¼" from the edges. Press the interfacing in place. Using a ¼" seam allowance, sew along the top, side, and bottom edges of the card, leaving a 2" opening on the long edge for turning. Clip across the corners and turn the card right side out. Slip-stitch the opening closed.

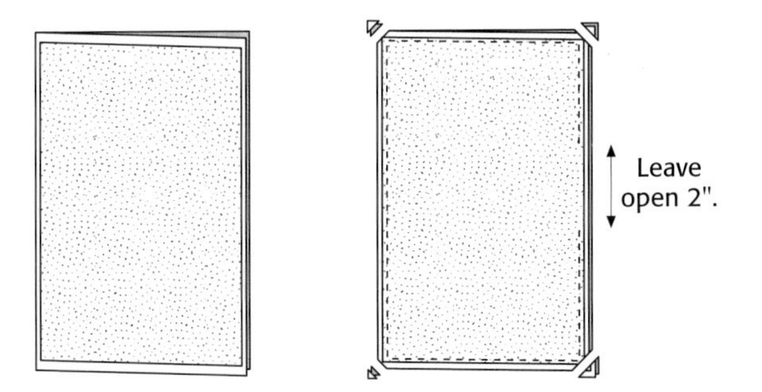

3. To make leaves for the ribbon rose, make a bow knot as follows. It is like tying your shoe but with just one string or lace. Double over the unattached end of the ribbon. Wrap the long end of the ribbon around the bend and push a loop under the wrap. Pull on the loops to make them equal, and then tighten the knot. If necessary, pull on the ribbon ends to adjust the loops and then tighten the knot again. Trim the short end to even up the loops.

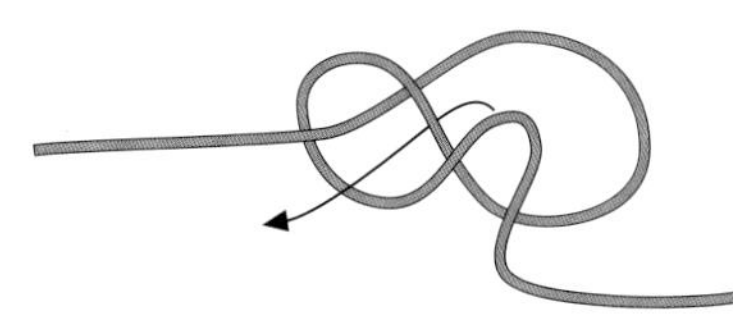

4. Stitch the bow to the upper corner of the card and then stitch the ribbon rose over the end of the ribbon. Fold the card in half and insert it into the envelope.

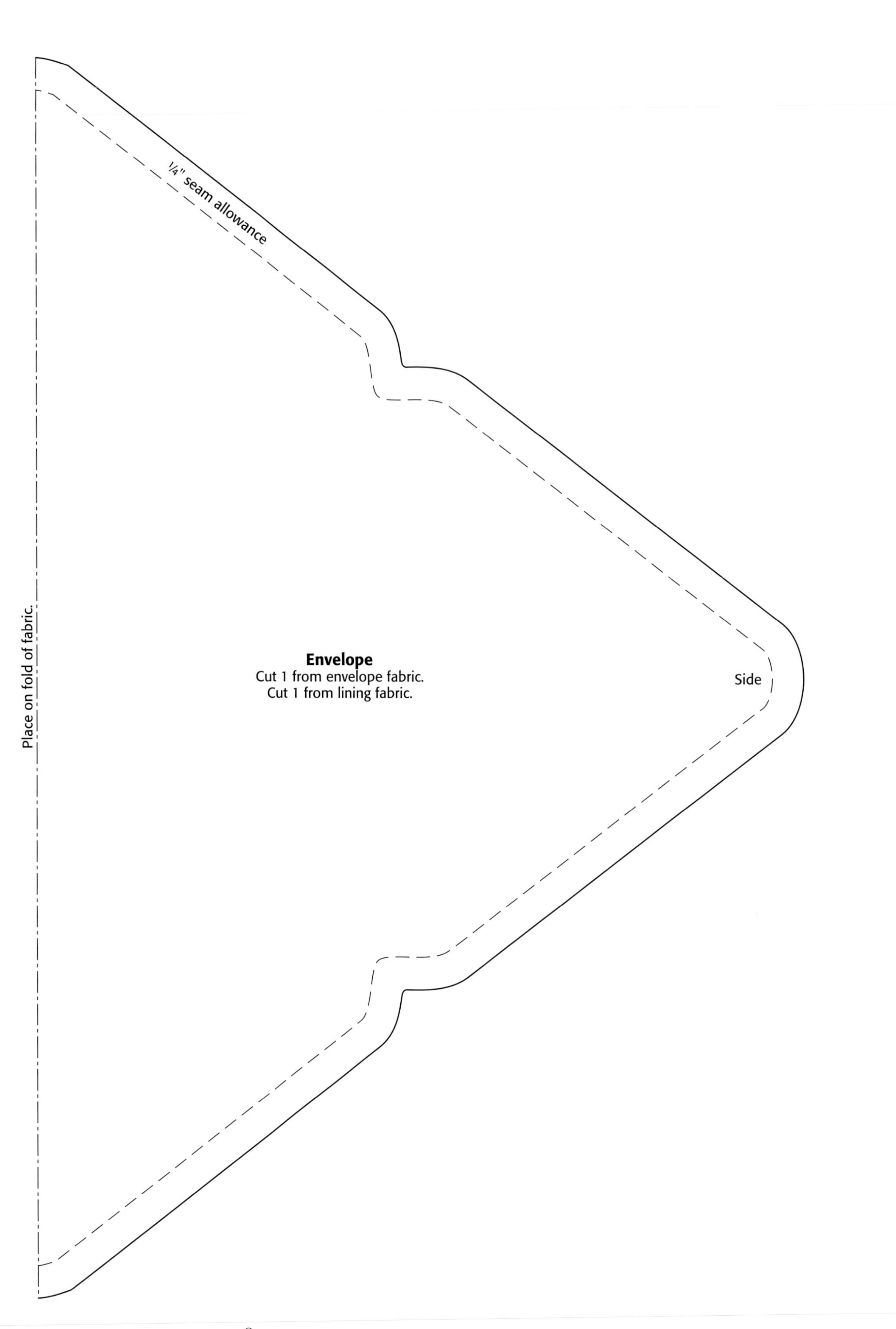
¼" seam allowance
Place on fold of fabric.
Envelope
Cut 1 from envelope fabric.
Cut 1 from lining fabric.
Side

CAKE-SLICE CARD WITH WEDDING CAKE POCKET

This is a great label for a wedding or anniversary quilt. The slice-of-cake card slides easily into the pocket, which is decorated on the front with a wedding cake.

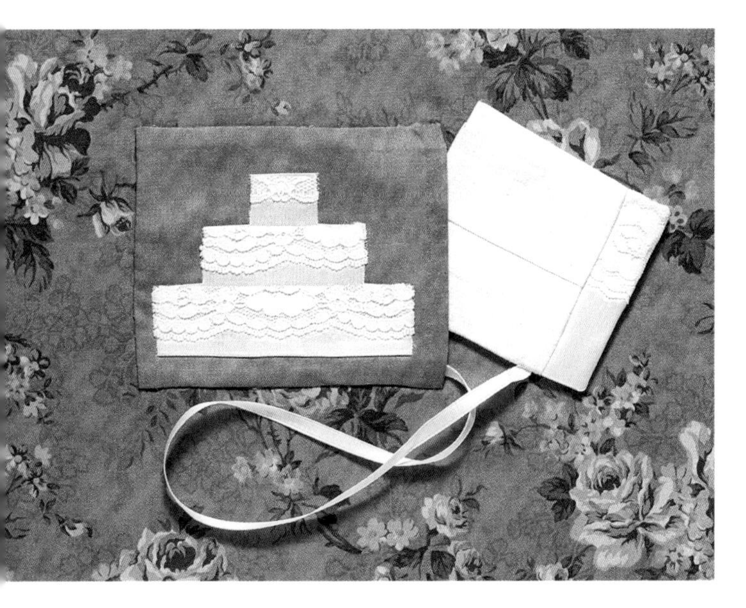

Dimensions: Pocket 4" x 5½", Card 4" x 3½"

Scraps of satin and lace make this label look like a slice of wedding cake.

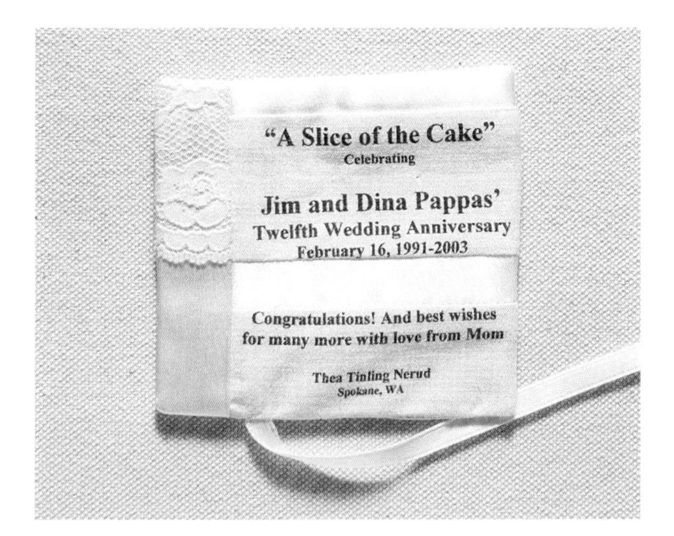

The lettered side of the slice-of-cake label shown above. I used homemade printable fabric for the lettered strips.

Materials

- 8½" x 11" piece of cream-colored, printable fabric ***or*** scraps of untreated cotton for card
- 4½" x 6" piece of solid fabric for pocket
- 6" x 12" piece of cream-colored satin for label and cake
- 15" length of 1"-wide scalloped lace
- 12" length of narrow satin ribbon for tether*
- Fusible web
- Freezer paper
- Teflon pressing sheet
- Permanent black marker

*I attach ribbon tethers to finished card and envelope pieces. If you'd prefer to hide one or more of the ribbon ends inside a seam, insert the ribbon between pieces of fabric when you sew them together.

Making the Card

Follow these steps to make a slice-of-wedding-cake label with a special message for the bride and groom.

1. Compose the label and letter the card fabric, referring to the lettering instructions on pages 15–23 as needed. The label shown at left was printed on a computer, and the lettering fits in two areas that measure 1¼" x 3½" each. If you want to computer-letter your label, leave several blank lines between the two lettering blocks to allow for seam allowances. If you want to accommodate more lettering on your label, refer to "Enlarging Patterns" on page 18 to enlarge the entire pattern.
2. Cut out the lettered areas to measure 1¾" x 4", which includes ¼" seam allowances. These pieces are the cake layers.

3. Cut two 1" x 4" strips of satin for the top and middle frosting layers. Stitch a satin strip to the top of each lettered strip and then sew the two units together. Press the seam allowances toward the printed pieces.

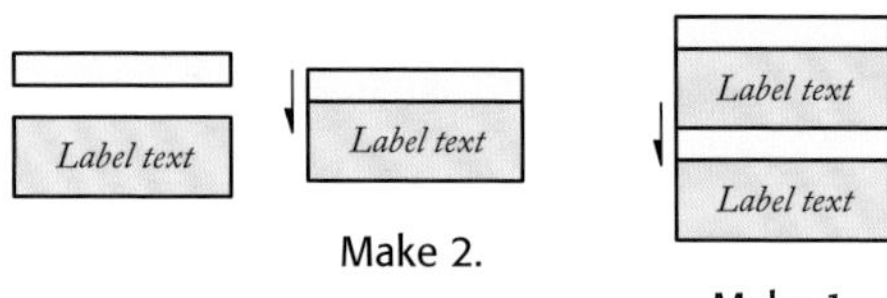

4. Cut two 1¾" x 4" unlettered pieces from the remaining cotton fabric. Cut two more 1" x 4" satin strips and sew them together as you did for the printed pieces.

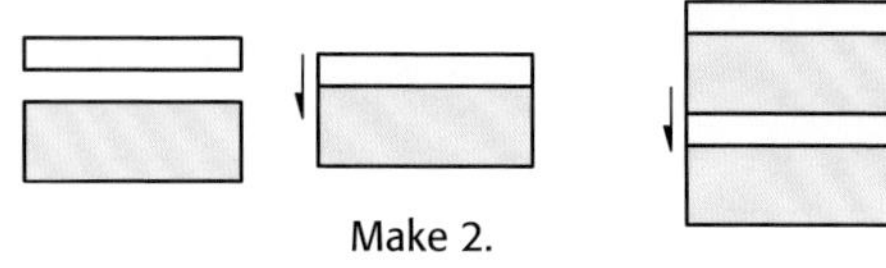

5. Cut two more 1" x 4" satin strips. Cut two 1"-wide pieces of lace. Fuse a lace piece across the top of each satin strip, aligning the upper edges and using the Teflon pressing sheet so that you don't get glue residue on your iron. Trim the lace even with the sides. Sew one of these strips to the left edge of the printed piece and the other strip to the right edge of the plain piece, as shown.

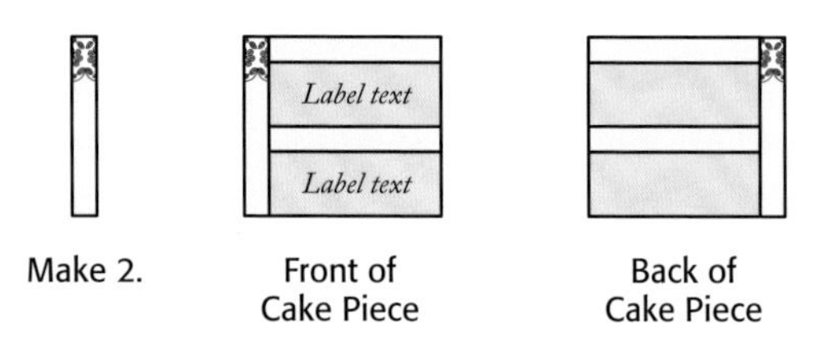

6. With right sides together, sew around the cake pieces, leaving an opening at the bottom for turning. Clip across the corners and turn the pieces right side out. Slip-stitch the opening closed. Press the completed label. Sew one end of the narrow ribbon tether to the side of the label.

Making the Pocket

Follow these steps to make a wedding-cake pocket that will delight the quilt's recipients.

1. On one short edge of the 4½" x 6" pocket rectangle, turn under a ¼" seam allowance twice. Stitch it in place. Turn under ¼" along the other three edges and press.

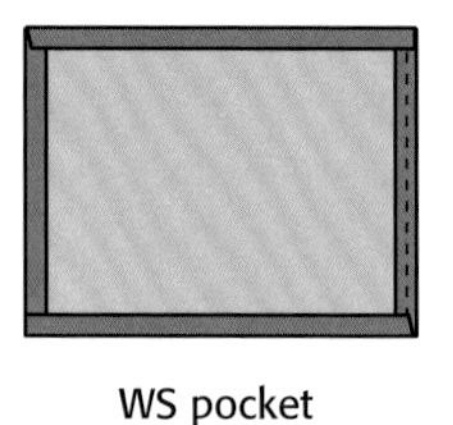

WS pocket

2. Trace the pattern for the wedding cake from page 51, including the seam allowances, onto freezer paper. Press the shiny side of the freezer-paper template onto the satin and cut out the wedding-cake shape. Clip the inner corners as shown. Remove the freezer paper. Cut lace strips long enough to go across the top of each layer, including ¼" seam allowances at the sides. For the middle layer, trim the ribbon to ¾" wide. For the top layer, trim the ribbon to ½" wide. Fuse the lace to the cake fabric, aligning the top of each lace piece with the top of its cake layer as shown. Turn under the top and bottom seam allowances and secure them with straight pins. Do the same for the sides of the cake layers.

3. Cut a piece of fusible web the size and shape of the cake minus seam allowances, and press this shape to the back of the cake. Remove the paper backing, position the cake on the fabric pocket, and fuse it in place. If you used lightweight fusible web, appliqué around the edges of the cake using your favorite method (see "Incorporating Appliqué Motifs" on pages 29–34 as needed).

4. Topstitch the three unhemmed edges of the pocket to the backing of your quilt. Sew the end of the ribbon tether inside the pocket. Slip the card into the pocket.

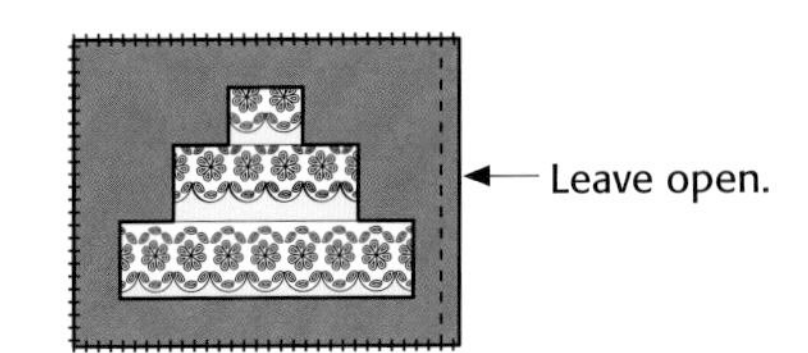

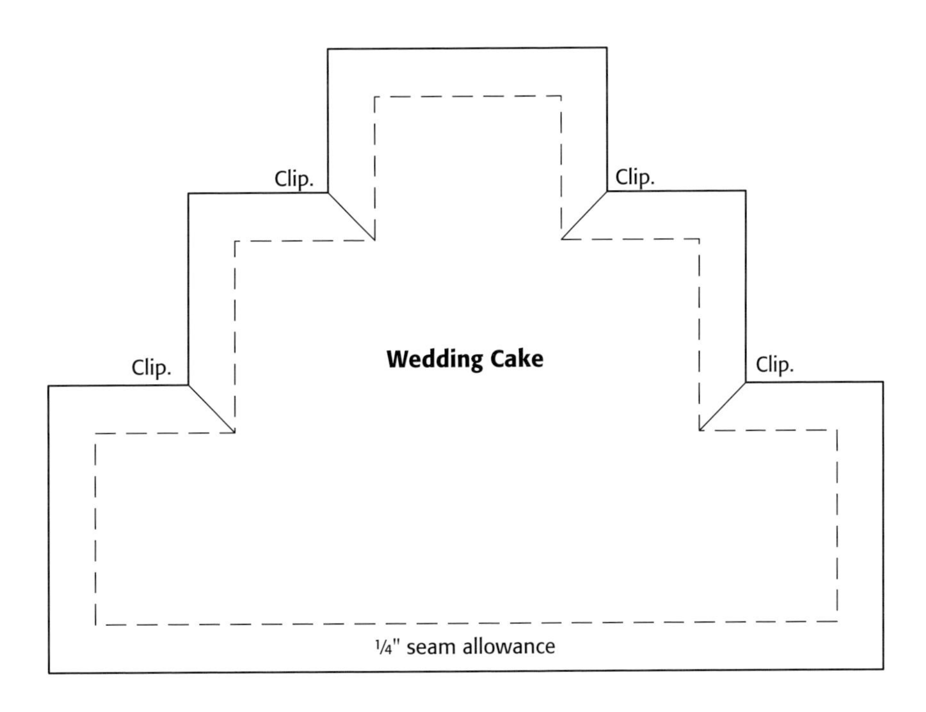

CAR CARD WITH GARAGE POCKET

OPEN THE garage door to see the car! Drive the car out of the garage to read the quilt label on the back. The car has a ribbon tether to keep it from straying too far. It's just the thing for folks who love vehicles.

DIMENSIONS: POCKET 7¾" x 6¼", CARD 5¾" x 3½"
Boys love just about anything with wheels. I made this for my grandson.

Materials

- 8½" x 11" piece of printable fabric or scrap of red, untreated cotton for car
- Scraps of black imitation suede ***or*** cotton fabric for tires. (If using cotton, you'll also need heavy, iron-on fusible web.)
- 9" x 9" square of gold fabric for lining
- 3" x 8" piece of fabric for roof
- 6½" x 8" piece of checked fabric for side and gable
- 6" x 6" square of gold fabric for door
- 3" x 6" piece of fusible interfacing
- Freezer paper
- Black permanent marker for marking freezer paper and car details (or use dimensional fabric paint for car details)
- Velcro dot closure
- 12" length of narrow ribbon for tether*

*I attach ribbon tethers to finished card and envelope pieces. If you'd prefer to hide one or more of the ribbon ends inside a seam, insert the ribbon between pieces of fabric when you sew them together.

The back of the car displays the quilt label.

Making the Car

Follow these steps to make a cute car label for a child's or baby's quilt, or for a quilt made for a car enthusiast.

1. Letter your text on the top half of the red fabric, referring to the lettering instructions on pages 15–23 as needed. The lettering in this pattern fits in a 1½" x 2¼" area. If you want to accommodate more lettering on your label, refer to "Enlarging Patterns" on page 18 to enlarge the entire label.

2. Using a photocopy machine, enlarge all of the car and garage patterns from page 55 by 125%. With the permanent marker, trace the patterns onto the uncoated side of freezer paper. Cut out the shapes on the marked lines.

3. Iron the shiny side of the car template to the *wrong* side of the lettered red fabric, positioning the pattern so that the text is centered inside the car. (You may have to hold the fabric and paper up to a bright light to see the position of the text.) Cut out the car, adding a ¼" seam allowance.

4. Remove the freezer-paper template from the car and iron it to the *right* side of the unlettered portion of the red fabric. Cut out the car piece, adding a ¼" seam allowance. The second car piece should be a mirror image of the first.

5. On both car pieces mark the tire placement, using the dashed lines on the car pattern as a guide. Without adding a seam allowance, cut a car piece from fusible interfacing. Press the interfacing piece to the wrong side of a fabric car. With right sides together, sew the two cars together, leaving an opening between the tire markings for turning. Clip the curves and corners, and turn the car right side out. Press. Slip-stitch the opening closed. Press.

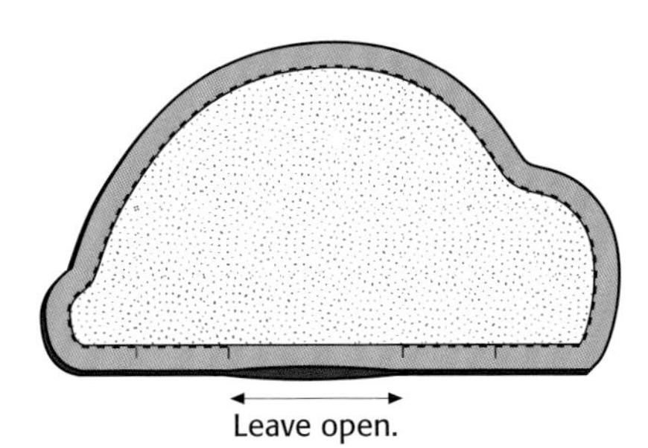

6. Cut four tires from imitation suede (or press heavy fusible web to the wrong side of black cotton and then cut out four tires). Position the tires on the car, pinning them in place (or fusing them in place if you used cotton). Make a narrow zigzag stitch in black thread around the edges, allowing the needle to just overlap the outer edges of the tires. The stitching will look like tire treads.

7. Pin the freezer-paper window and door templates in place on the car. Using the permanent marker or dimensional fabric paint, outline the windows, door, and door handle. Freehand outline the bumpers and headlight. Sew one end of the narrow ribbon to the rear bumper.

Making the Pocket

Follow these steps to make the garage pocket.

1. Trace the garage patterns from page 55 onto the uncoated side of freezer paper and cut them out on the marked lines. Press the shiny sides of the templates to the wrong sides of the fabrics for the side, gable, and roof. Cut out the pieces, adding ¼" seam allowances around each. Remove the freezer paper.

2. Fold the door fabric right sides together and press the shiny side of the freezer-paper template to the wrong side of the fabric, leaving at least ¼" of fabric all around the pattern. Pin to stabilize the template and cut around the shape, ¼" from the edges, through both layers of fabric. Remove the freezer paper.

Cut shape, adding ¼" seam allowances.

3. Sew the roof piece to the gable, matching points A and B, and press the seam allowance toward the roof. On the right edge of the garage's side, turn under ¼" twice and stitch to hem. Sew the top of the garage's side to the lower edge of the roof, aligning the hemmed edge with the seam junction of the roof and gable pieces.

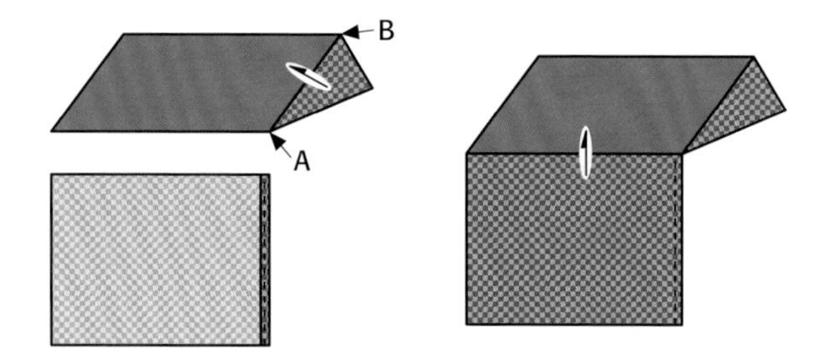

4. Without adding seam allowances, cut two door pieces (one regular and one reversed), from fusible interfacing and press each to the wrong side of a fabric door. With right sides together, sew the door pieces together, leaving the upper edge open for turning. Clip the corners, turn the door right side out, and press. Sew the top of the door to the bottom of the gable, aligning the corners as shown.

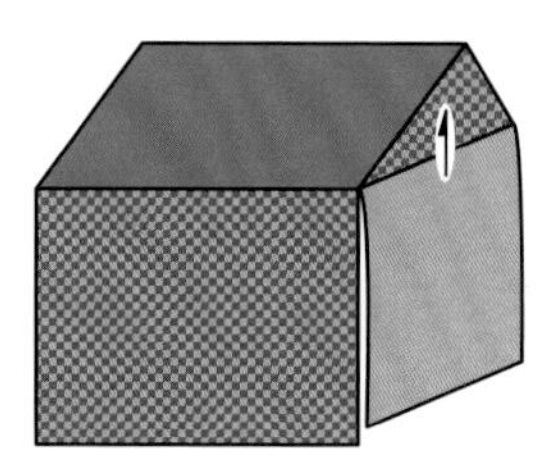

5. With right sides up, place the garage on the 9" gold square, aligning the left and bottom edges. Pin in place. Using a ⅛" seam allowance, sew the lining and garage together along the bottom, left, top, and gable edges. Be careful not to catch the door in your stitching.

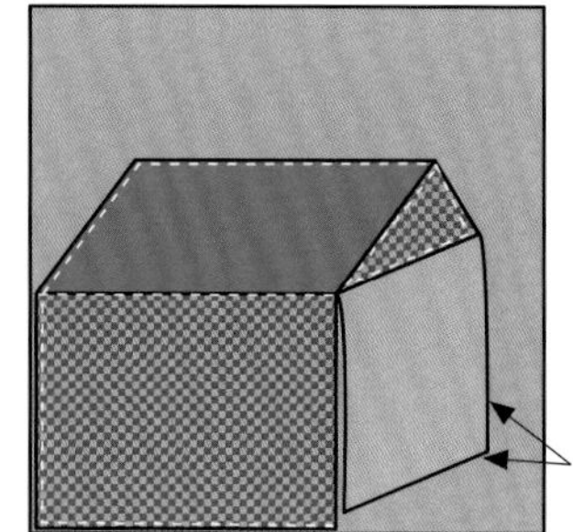

6. Where you stitched, trim the lining even with the garage pieces. Trim the lining behind the door, leaving ¼" seam allowances. Lift the door and pin it out of the way. Fold under the edges of the garage, and the lining behind the garage door, by ¼".

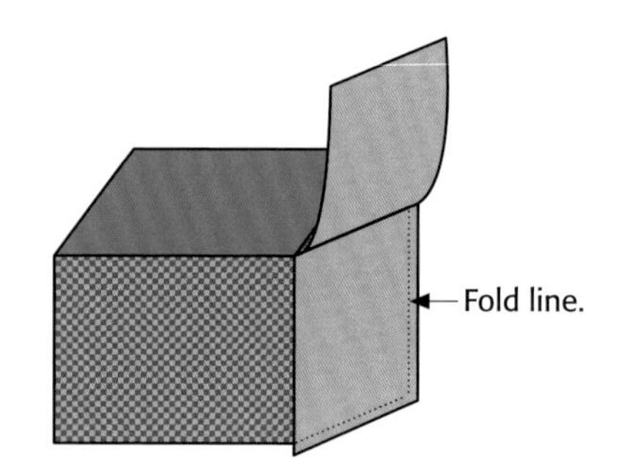

7. Pin the garage pocket in place on the completed quilt back, and appliqué or topstitch it in place. Stitch half of a Velcro dot to the inside bottom of the door and stitch the other half to the lining beneath it. Sew one end of the narrow ribbon to the inside of the garage.

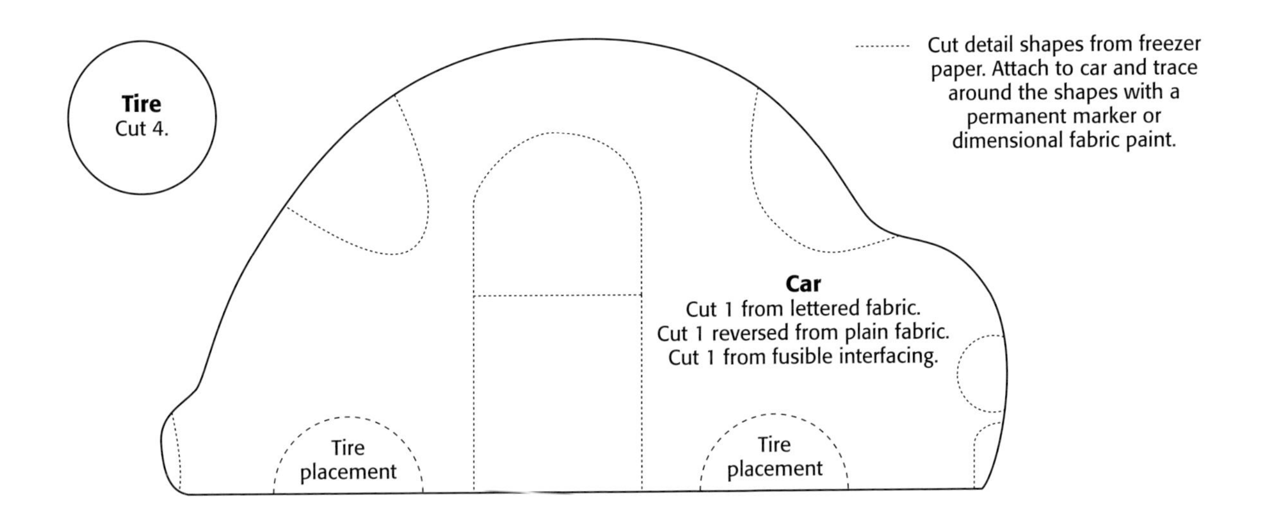

Enlarge all patterns on this page 125%.

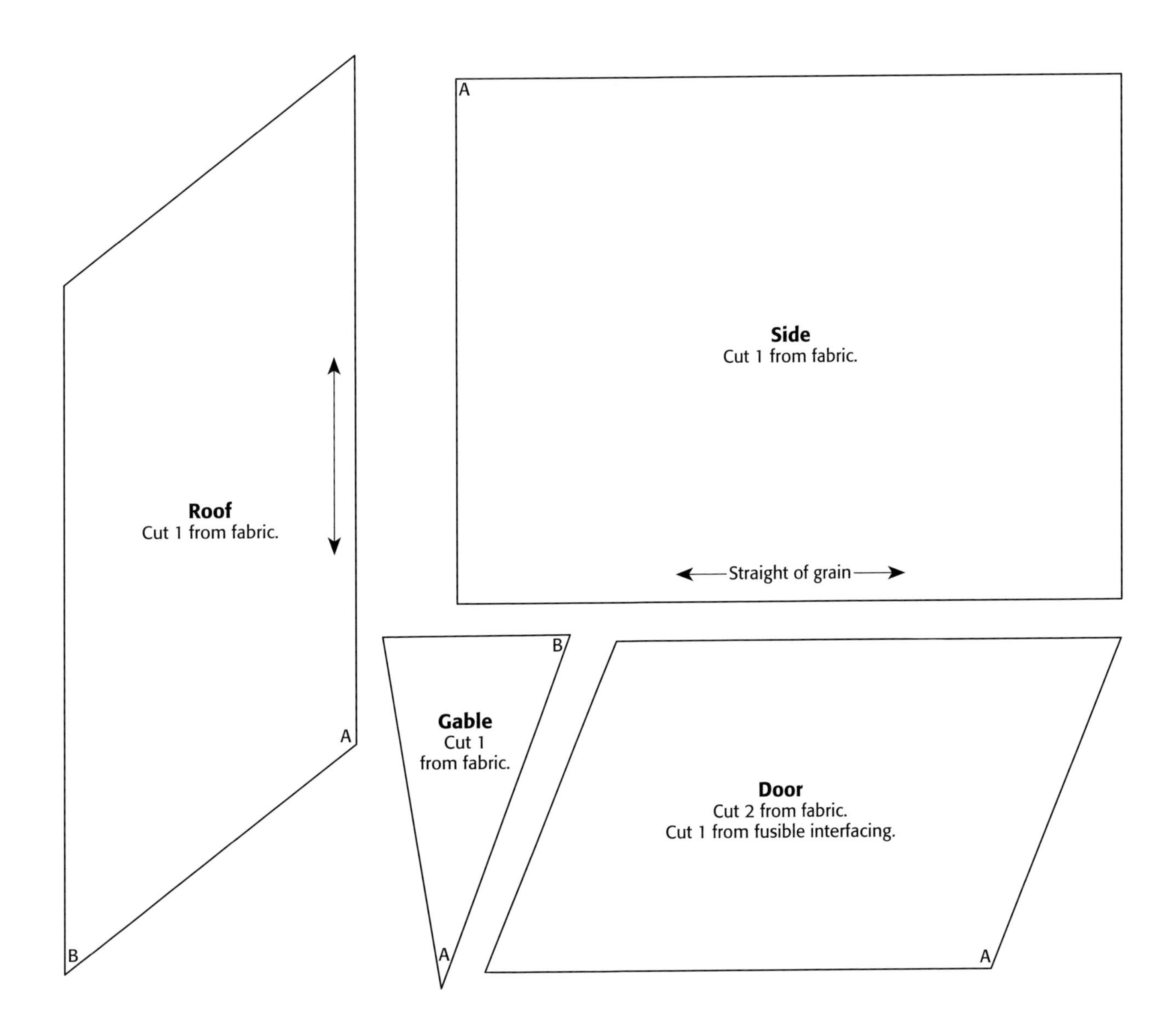

KERCHIEF CARD WITH JEANS POCKET

I'M MAKING a quilt from my children's old jeans. I cut out the pocket from one pair and made a kerchief card for the label.

DIMENSIONS: POCKET 5½" x 6", CARD 3½" x 7"

Materials

- White fabric for label. (Use printable fabric or untreated cotton fabric as needed for your chosen lettering method.)
- 9" x 9" square of red kerchief fabric
- Jeans pocket with lining*
- 12" length of narrow red ribbon for tether**
- 3½" x 7" piece of fusible interfacing

*Cut a pocket from a pair of jeans, leaving the lining intact and ½" of denim fabric around the pocket edges.
**I attach ribbon tethers to finished card and envelope pieces. If you'd prefer to hide one or more of the ribbon ends inside a seam, insert the ribbon between pieces of fabric when you sew them together.

Making the Card

1. Letter your text on the white fabric, formatting the lettering to fit a 2½" x 2½" area. Refer to the lettering instructions on pages 15–23 as needed. If you want to accommodate more lettering on your label, refer to "Enlarging Patterns" on page 18 to resize the entire pattern.
2. Cut the lettered fabric into a 3" square, centering the text and making sure that the edges are straight and square with the lettering.
3. Cut two 1" x 3" strips of kerchief fabric. Using a ¼" seam allowance, sew the kerchief strips to the sides of the label. Press the seam allowances toward the kerchief fabric. Cut a 1" x 4" strip of kerchief fabric and sew it to the bottom of the label. Press the seam allowance toward the kerchief fabric.
4. Cut a 4" x 4½" square of kerchief fabric and sew it to the top of the unit from step 3. Press the seam allowance toward the kerchief fabric.
5. Cut a 4" x 7½" piece of kerchief fabric. Center the 3½" x 7" piece of interfacing on the fabric and fuse it in place, following the interfacing manufacturer's instructions. Place the fused fabric on top of the label unit, with right sides together. Sew around the edges, using a ¼" seam allowance and leaving an opening on one side for turning. Clip the corners and turn the card right side out. Slip-stitch the opening closed. Attach one end of the narrow ribbon to the edge of the card.

Making the Pocket

Position the jeans pocket on your quilt backing. Turn under the ½" seam allowances around the edges and pin the pocket in place. Stitch the pocket to the quilt back by hand or machine, referring to "Incorporating Appliqué Motifs" on page 29. Sew the other end of the ribbon to the inside of the pocket. Fold the kerchief card in half and slip it into the pocket.

TRAIN CARD WITH TUNNEL POCKET

This train label was inspired by a juvenile-print fabric. The train is the card, and a tunnel becomes the pocket. A ribbon tether keeps the train from getting lost. Let your imagination soar when you look through novelty prints in your local quilt shop.

Dimensions: Pocket 10" x 7", Card 6" x 4"

For all the train lovers in the world. Let novelty prints inspire you.

Materials

- Backing fabric for quilt to be labeled
- Scrap of novelty print for label motif. (If your motif is larger than 4¼" x 6¼", you might need to enlarge the tunnel pocket. See "Enlarging Patterns" on page 18.)
- Label printed on iron-on transfer film (see "Iron-on Transfer Film" on page 20), sized to fit on the back of your novelty-print motif*
- Scrap of fabric for lining
- 6" x 8" piece of light gray for tunnel front
- 8" x 8" square of dark gray for inner tunnel wall
- 11" x 11" square of rock print for roadbed
- Freezer paper
- Black and brown permanent markers
- 12" length of narrow ribbon for tether**
- Air-soluble marker

*If you prefer, make a fabric label that will fit on your novelty-print motif and then stitch it to the back of the finished motif.

**I attach ribbon tethers to finished card and envelope pieces. If you'd prefer to hide one or more of the ribbon ends inside a seam, insert the ribbon between pieces of fabric when you sew them together.

The lettered label on the back of the train card shown above

The train fabric used in the label

Making the Card

Follow these steps to make the train card.

1. Cut a motif from the novelty print, leaving a ¼" seam allowance around the edges. With right sides together, place the motif on top of the lining fabric and cut the lining to match.
2. Using a ¼" seam allowance, sew around the edges of the figure and lining, leaving an opening along the bottom for turning. Clip any corners and curves and turn the figure right side out. Slip-stitch the opening closed.
3. Press the label onto the back of the motif, referring to "Iron-on Transfer Film" on page 20.

Making the Pocket

Follow these steps to make the pocket.

1. Using a permanent marker, trace the pattern pieces for the tunnel and roadbed from pages 59–60 onto the uncoated side of freezer paper and cut them out on the drawn lines. Using a hot, dry iron, press the templates to the wrong sides of the corresponding fabrics. Cut out the pieces, adding ¼" seam allow-ances. Using the air-soluble marker, mark the curve of the tunnel and the dots on the fabric pieces.
2. Determine the position of the tunnel face on your quilt backing. Place the *right* side of the tunnel fabric against the *wrong* side of the quilt backing and pin the tunnel in place. Stitch along the inner curve from dot to dot, as shown. Cut through the quilt backing along the curved seam allowance of the tunnel piece. Also cut from dot to dot across the bottom of the tunnel opening. Turn the tunnel face fabric through the opening to the right side of the quilt backing. Turn under ¼" along the outer edges and topstitch them in place.

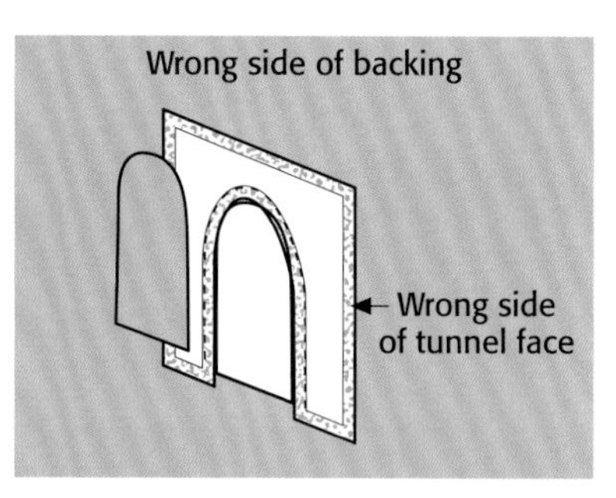

Stitch inner curve of tunnel face.
Cut tunnel opening in backing fabric.

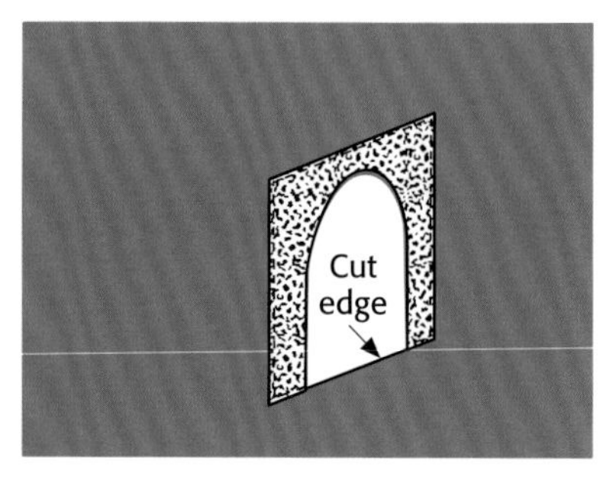

Turn tunnel face to right side of backing.
Turn under seam allowance and topstitch.

3. Sew the tunnel wall to the roadbed; then open the seam allowance and press it flat. Position the inside of the tunnel under the quilt backing, and bring the end of the roadbed out through the tunnel opening. Match mark 1 with the seam in the tunnel wall and pin the entire piece to the quilt backing. Turn under the edges of the roadbed in front of the tunnel, and pin it in place. Topstitch the right edge of the tunnel opening from mark 2 to the bottom, and continue topstitching around the edges of the roadbed.

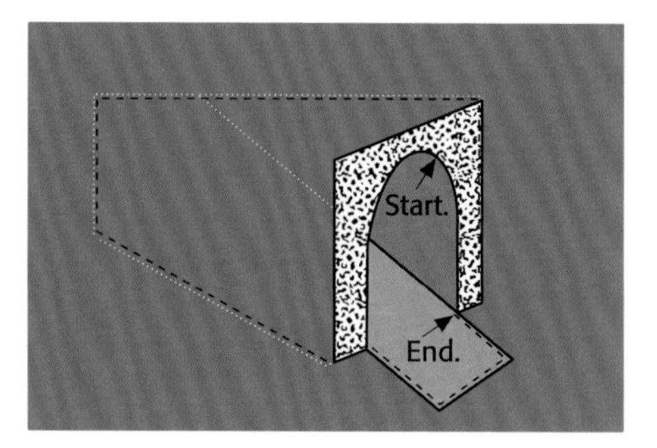

Topstitch around edges.

4. Spread the pocket (the inside of the tunnel) flat under the backing fabric. Pin it in place from the back and then stitch around the pocket. Do not sew over the tunnel face.
5. Sew one end of the ribbon to the back of the train and the other end inside the tunnel.
6. Draw rails on the roadbed with the black permanent marker. Draw railroad ties on the roadbed with the brown marker. Be careful not to quilt through the tunnel pocket when you finish the quilt.

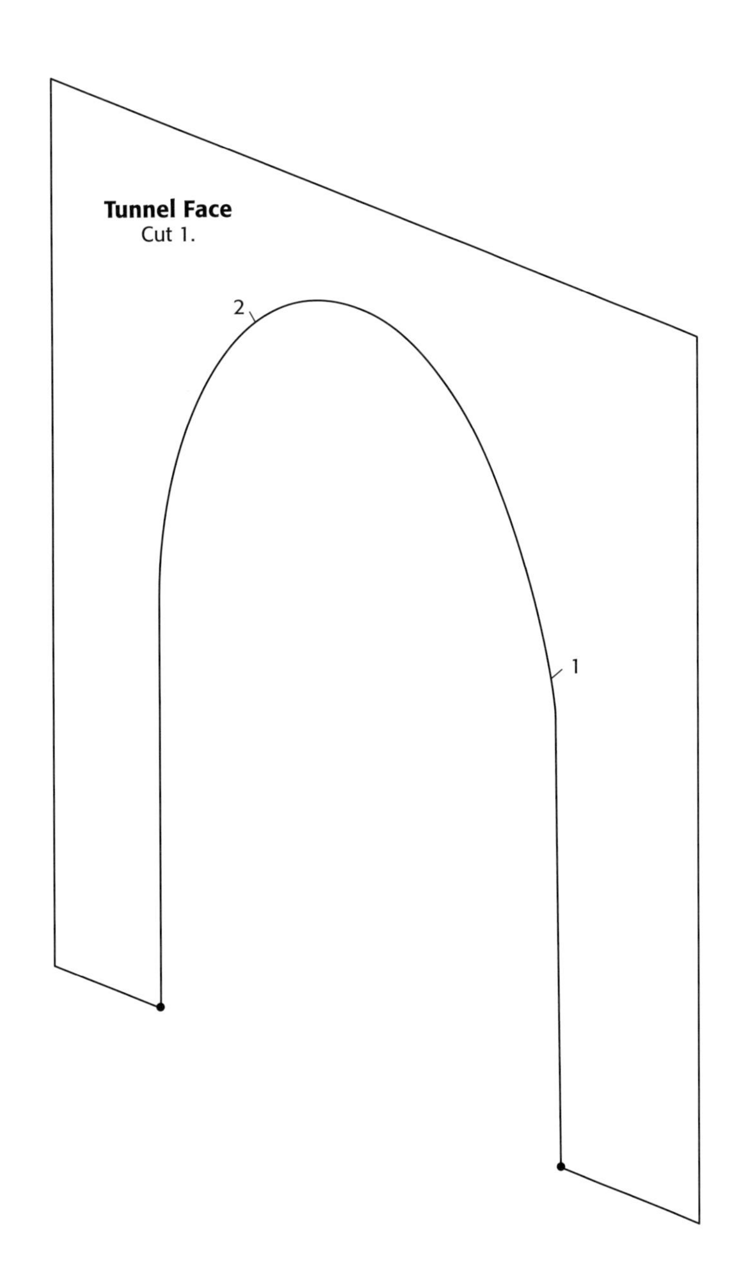

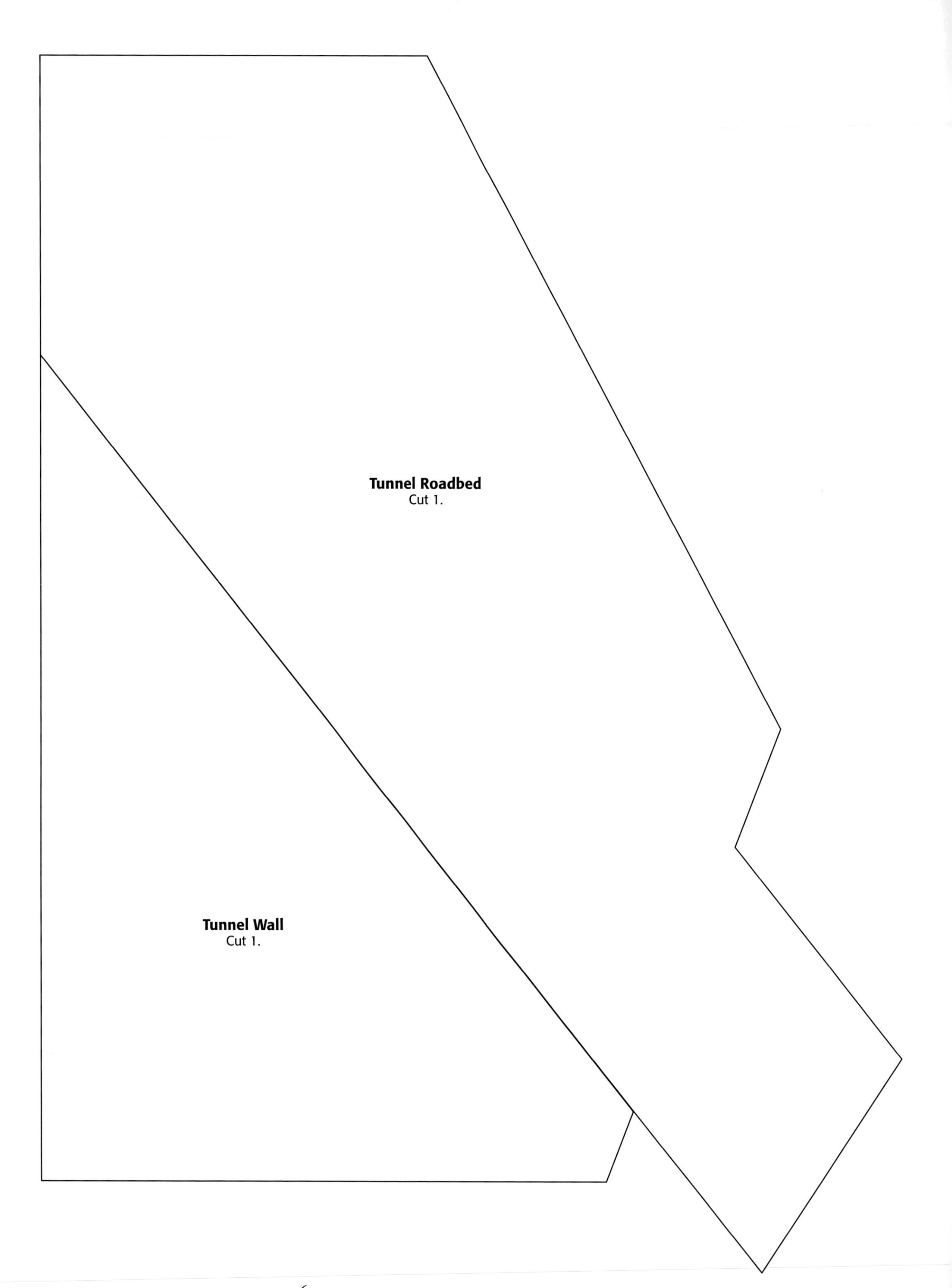
Tunnel Roadbed
Cut 1.
Tunnel Wall
Cut 1.

Special Labels for Children

When making a label for a baby or child's quilt, let your sense of whimsy take over. Experiment with dimensional elements and textured fabrics to make your labels fun for kids.

Dimensions: 3" x 4½"
Gingham Dog, Calico Cat, Bunny, and Teddy Bear labels

ANIMAL LABELS

Each animal label has a 3" x 3" space for lettering. If your text won't fit into a space of this size, enlarge the label as desired, referring to "Enlarging Patterns" on page 18.

Materials

- Scrap (at least 6" x 6") of cotton fabric for background
- Scrap of cotton fabric for face
- Scrap of imitation suede for ears
- Fine-point permanent marker

Making the Label

Follow these steps to make an animal label.

1. Cut a 3½" x 3½" square of background fabric. Compose your label and letter the square, referring to the lettering instructions on pages 15–23 as needed.
2. Cut a 1½" x 1½" square from the face fabric.
3. Make ears as follows.

For the dog: Cut two ½" x 1" pieces of imitation suede for the ears. Cut a curve along the short end of each ear piece (for a full-size pattern, see the cutting guide on page 63). Make a pleat in each ear and pin to the face square at an angle as shown. Stay stitch ⅛" from the top of the square to secure.

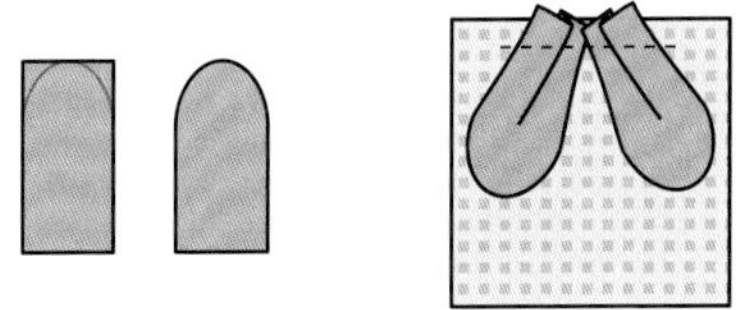

For the cat: Referring to the cutting guide on page 63, cut two ears from imitation suede. Make a pleat in the long side of each ear. Pin the pleated ears to the face square, making sure that the ears don't overlap the side seam allowances. Stay stitch ⅛" from the top of the square to secure. If any suede extends past the seam allowance, trim it even with the square.

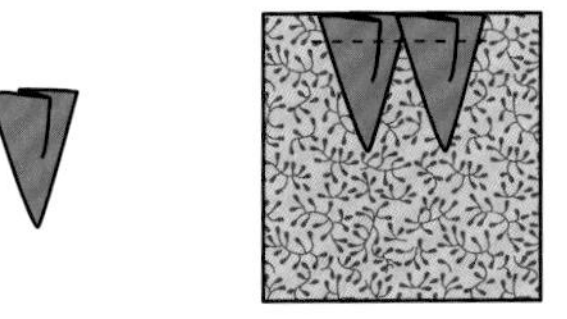

For the bunny: Cut two ½" x 1½" strips of imitation suede for the ears. Layer the suede strips and, using a pair of sharp scissors, cut a rounded point at one end (for a full-size pattern, see the cutting guide on page 63). Pin the ears to the right side of the face square, aligning the straight edges as shown and making a pleat in each ear. Stay stitch ⅛" from the top of the square to secure.

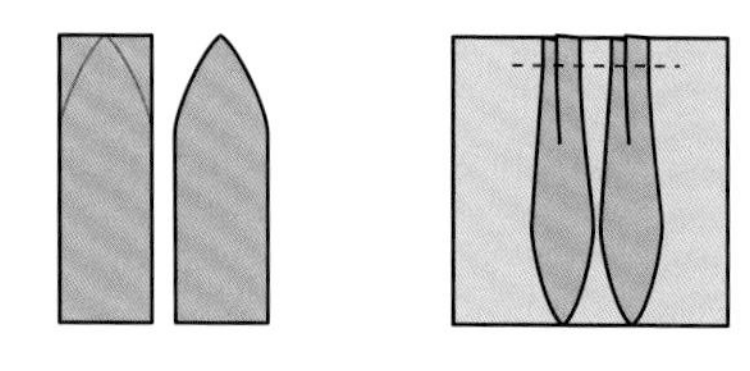

Making Bunny Ears from Cotton Fabric

To make ears from cotton fabric rather than from imitation suede, cut two 1½" squares of fabric, fold each in half, and draw a rounded point at one narrow end with an air-soluble marker. Using a short machine stitch (12 to 14 stitches per inch), sew ⅛" from a lower edge up to the point and then down the other side, leaving the bottom open. Trim the seam allowance around the pointed end to ⅛", turn the ear right side out, and press. Pin the ears in place at the top of the face, making a small pleat in each. Stay stitch ⅛" from the upper edge of the face to secure.

For the teddy bear: Cut two ⅝" x ⅝" squares of imitation suede for the ears. Cut a curve on each square as shown (for a full-size pattern, see the cutting guide on page 63). Make a pleat in the straight edge of each ear and pin the ears to the sides of the square. Stay stitch ⅛" from the sides of the square to secure.

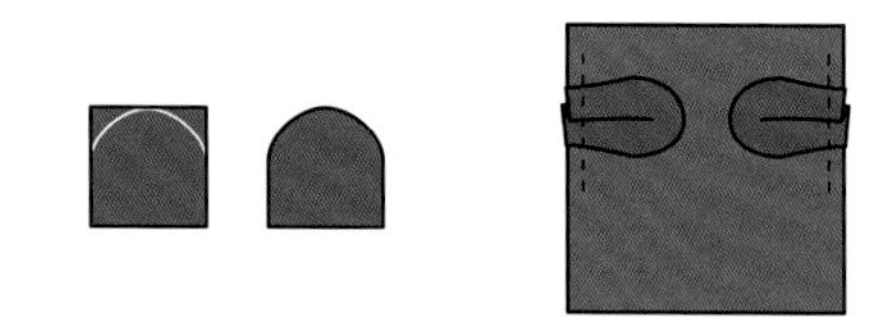

4. Cut a 1¼" x 2" strip of background fabric. With right sides together, place the strip against the face square so that the upper edges align and the sides of the strip overhang the square. Using a ¼" seam allowance, stitch the strip to the square. Trim the strip even with the sides of the face and ¾" from the seam. (Trimming an oversized piece produces the best results.) For the dog and teddy bear, press the seam allowance away from the face. For the bunny and cat, press the seam allowance toward the face to make the ears stand up.

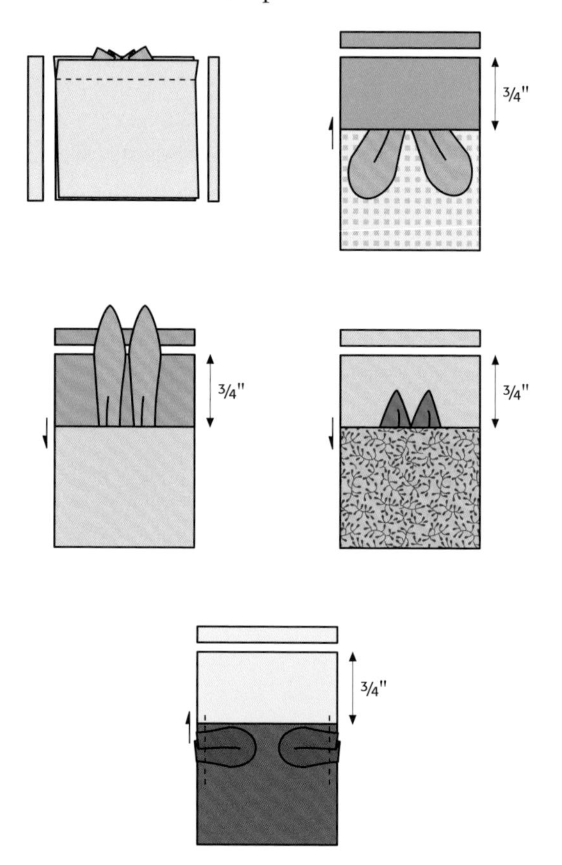

5. Cut two 1½"-wide background strips and sew them to the sides of the face unit, trimming the ends even with the top and the bottom of the unit. For the dog, cat, and bunny, press the seam allowance away from the face. For the teddy bear, press the seam allowance toward the face. Sew the 3½" square of lettered background fabric to the

bottom of the face unit. Press the seam allowances toward the background.

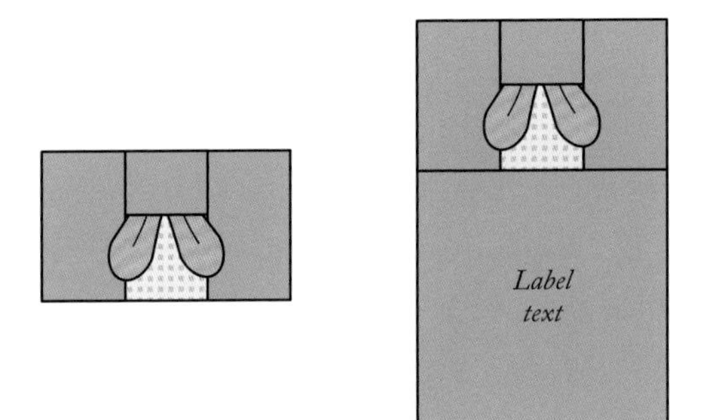

6. Using the permanent marker, draw the features on the face, referring to the placement guides as shown. Turn under ¼" on all sides of the label and press. Attach the label to the backing of your quilt, referring to "Incorporating Appliqué Motifs" on pages 29–34.

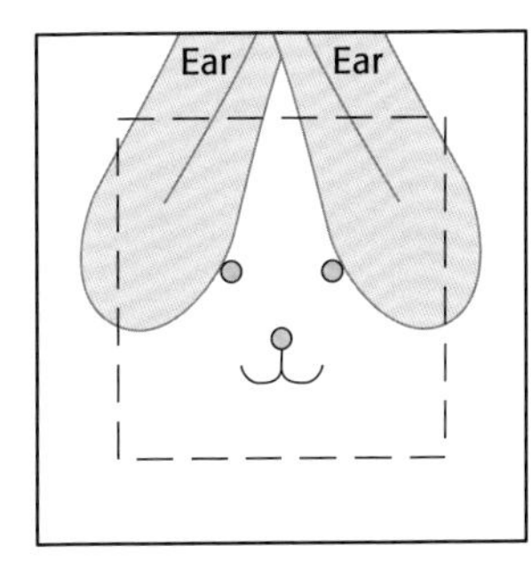

Gingham Dog Placement Guide

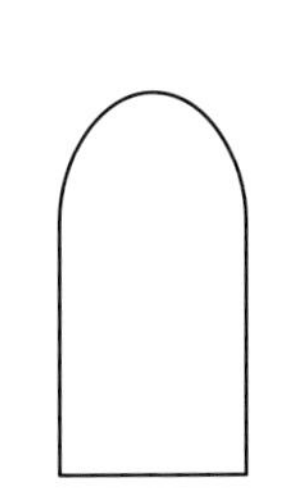
Ear Cutting Guide

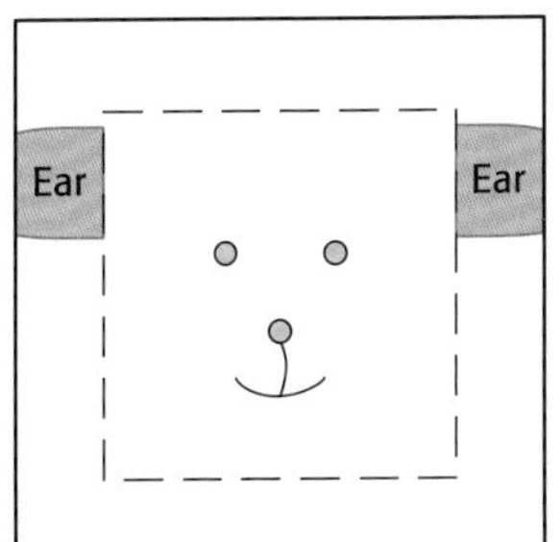

Teddy Bear Placement Guide

Ear Cutting Guide

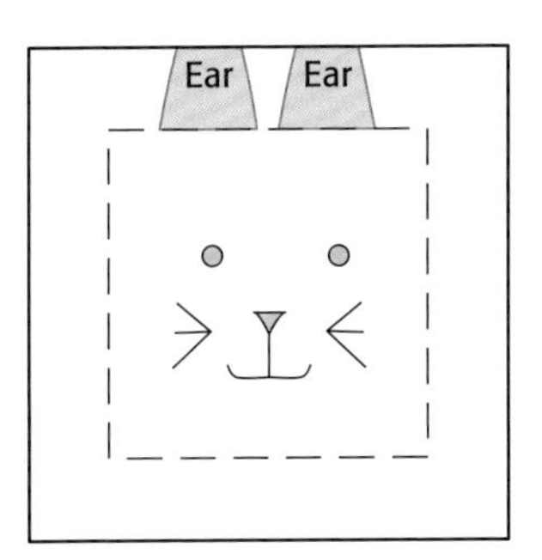

Calico Cat Placement Guide

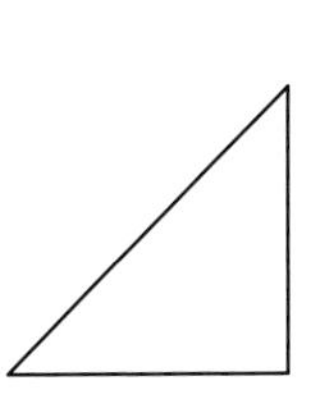
Ear Cutting Guide

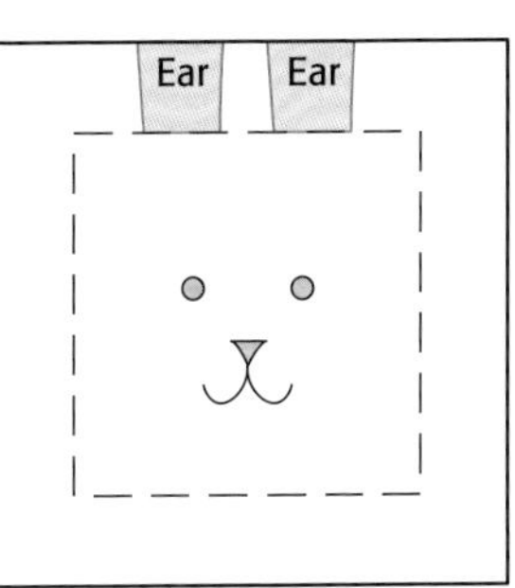

Bunny Placement Guide

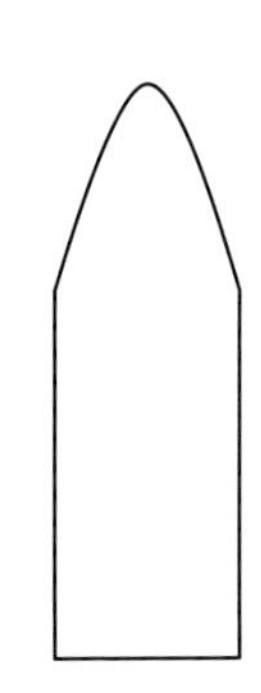
Ear Cutting Guide

ITTY-BITTY BUDDIES

WHAT COULD be cuter than a bunny label? Only one that also features some of the bunny's buddies! Follow these steps to make a label with three tiny animals.

DIMENSIONS: 5" DIAMETER

A Gingham Dog, Calico Cat, and Teddy Bear share a label.

Materials

- 3 animal faces (see step 1 at right)
- Scrap of tan for background, at least 9" x 9"
- Scrap of tan for label
- Fine-point permanent marker
- Freezer paper

Making the Label

Follow these steps to make a label featuring three different animals.

1. Cut a 2¾" x 5½" tan rectangle. Compose your label and letter the rectangle within a 1½" x 3" area, referring to the lettering instructions on pages 15–23 as needed.
2. Make three animal faces with ears, referring to the instructions on pages 61–63. Don't mark the faces yet. The teddy bear ears shown in the photo are sewn to the top of the face square instead of to the sides.
3. From the tan fabric for background, cut three squares, 1½" x 1½"; two rectangles, 1½" x 2½"; and one rectangle, 1½" x 5½".
4. Sew the three 1½" tan squares and two animal faces into a row, alternating the squares and faces and starting and ending with a tan square. Press the seam allowances away from the faces. Sew the third animal face between the 1½" x 2½" rectangles. Press the seam allowances away from the face. Sew the two rows together. For my label, I pressed the seam allowance open, clipping the seam allowance to make the dog's ears flop down and the cat's ears stick up.

5. Sew the 1½" x 5½" tan rectangle to the top of the unit from step 4. Press the seam allowance toward the face.
6. Sew the 2¾" x 5½" lettered piece to the bottom of the animal unit. Press the seam allowance away from the faces. Add markings to the faces with the fine-point permanent marker.

7. Using a permanent marker, trace the circle below onto the uncoated side of freezer paper and cut it out on the line. With the shiny side down, center the paper circle over the label, leaving a ½" margin around the text. Cut out the circle ¼" from the edge of the paper. Turn and press the ¼" seam allowance around the circle. Remove the freezer paper. Attach the label to the backing of your quilt with a machine blanket stitch.

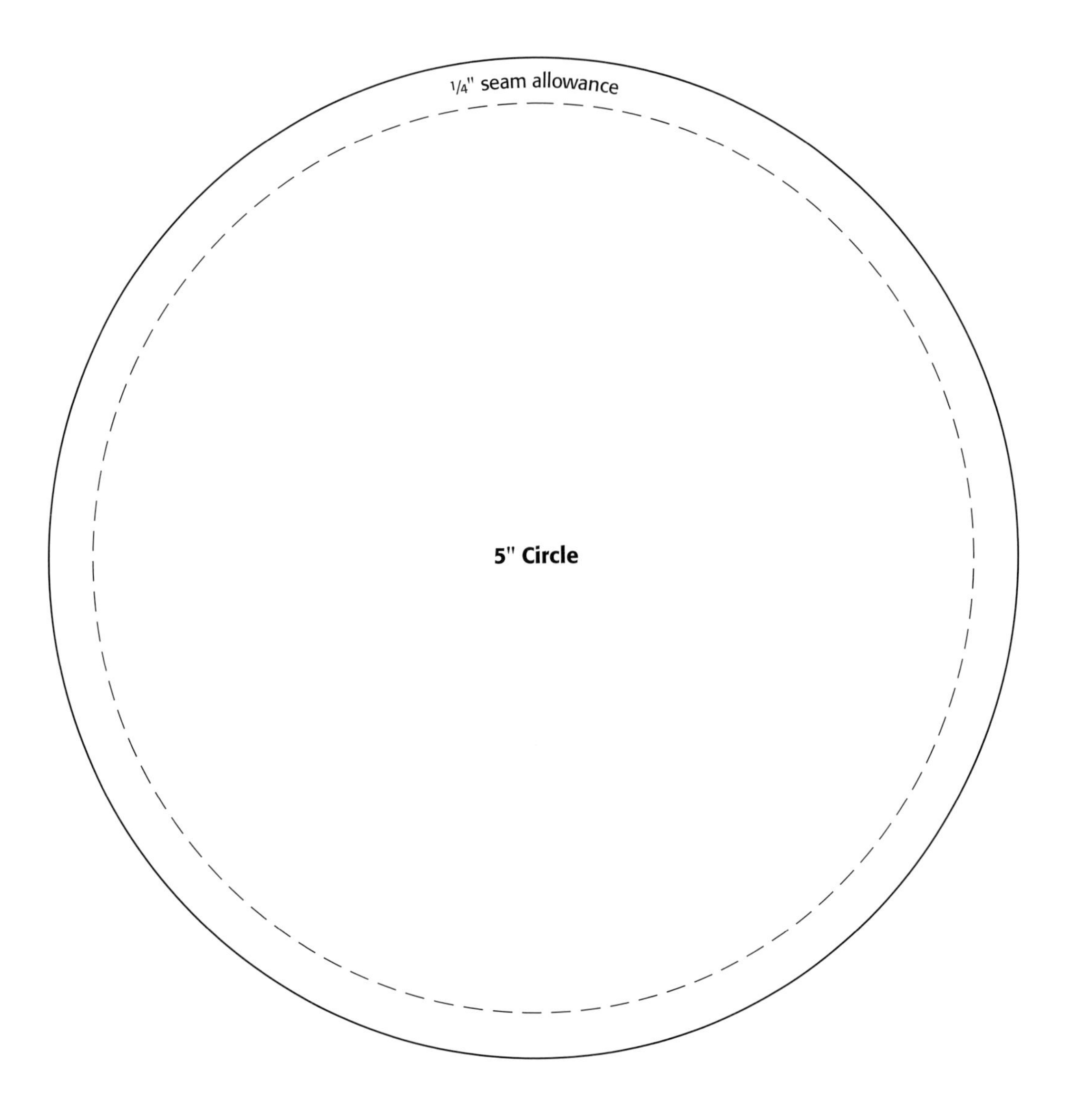

BABY BUNNY BUNTING

PERFECT FOR your next baby quilt, here is a baby bunny all snug in its bunting.

DIMENSIONS: 4" x 6"

I originally made this label for a baby quilt given to a neighbor. I re-created the label for this book.

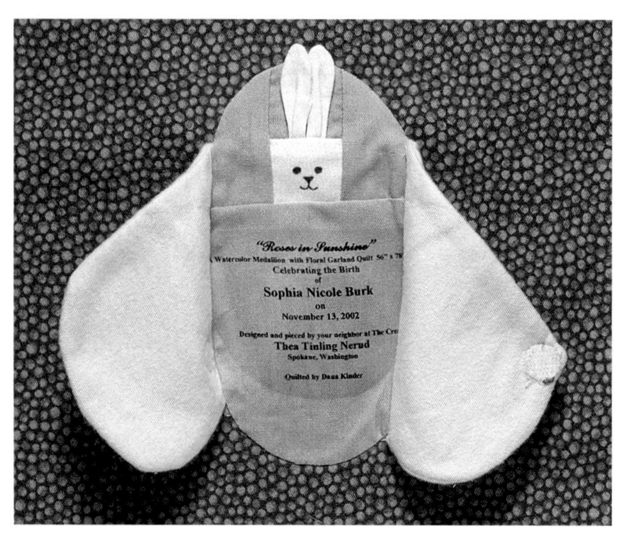

Open the blanket to read the label.

Materials

- 1 bunny face (see step 1 below)
- Scraps of green cotton for background
- ⅛ yard of pink flannel for blanket
- Narrow pink and green ribbon, each in a 12" length, for silk-ribbon rose with leaves
- ½" Velcro dot closure
- Freezer paper
- Fine-point permanent marker for drawing face
- Medium-point permanent marker for tracing onto freezer paper
- Pencil or air-soluble marker

Making the Label

Follow these steps to make a baby bunny label.

1. Make a bunny face with ears, referring to "Animal Labels" on page 61. The ears on my label were made with fabric instead of imitation suede.
2. Compose your label, formatting it to fit in a 3¼" x 3¼" space. If your message is too large for an area of this size, enlarge the label pattern as desired, referring to "Enlarging Patterns" on page 18. Letter the square, referring to the lettering instructions on pages 15–23 as needed.
3. Using a black permanent marker, trace the pattern pieces from page 68 onto the uncoated side of freezer paper, including the X marks and numbered hatch marks. Cut out the pieces on the marked lines.
4. Press the shiny side of the top, left-side, and right-side templates to the wrong side of the green fabric. Press the text-area pattern to the wrong side of the lettered label, centering the text.

5. Fold the pink flannel in half, right sides together, and press the shiny sides of the left and right blanket-flap patterns to the wrong side of the pink flannel. Using the pencil or air-soluble marker, transfer all marks and numbers from the templates to the fabric seam allowances. Adding ¼" seam allowances, cut around all of the templates.
6. Sew the top piece to the bunny face, pressing the seam allowances toward the face to make the bunny's ears stand up. Sew the side pieces to the face, pressing the seam allowances toward the sides.
7. Sew the lettered fabric to the bottom of the face unit. Press the seam allowance toward the label. Add markings to the bunny's face with the fine-point permanent marker.

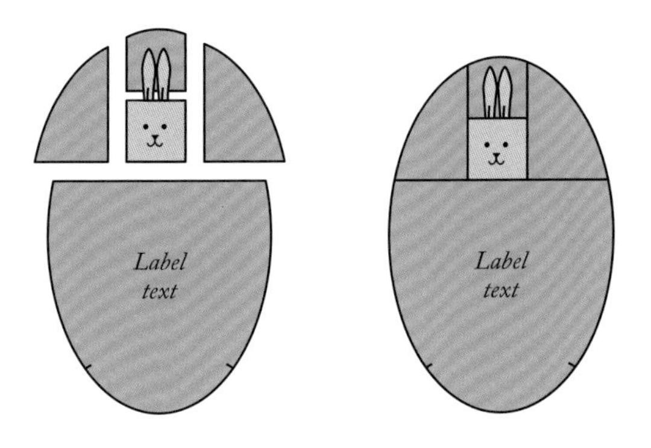

8. With right sides together, sew the right blanket-flap pieces together, using a ¼" seam allowance and leaving the flaps unstitched between marks 1 and 2. Clip the seam allowance along the curves, turn the piece right side out, and press. Repeat to make the left flap, leaving the edges unstitched between marks 3 and 4.
9. Pin the right blanket flap to the edge of the label, matching mark 2 and aligning the raw edges. Pin the left blanket flap to the edge of the label, matching mark 4 and aligning the raw edges. Stay stitch ⅛" from the raw edges on both flaps.

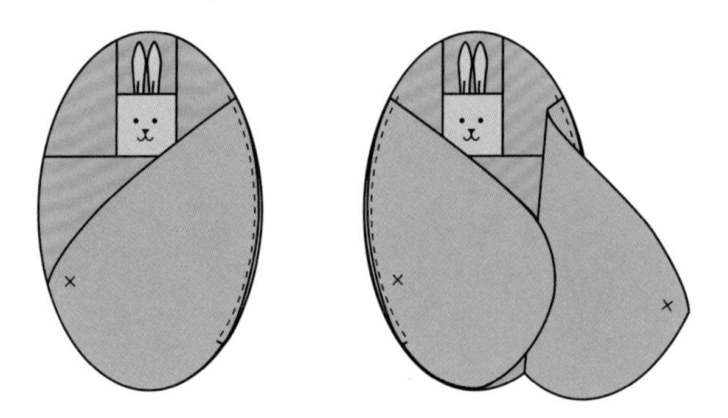

10. Securely sew one Velcro dot inside the right blanket flap at the X mark. Sew the other dot to the outside of the left flap. Turn under the edges of the label and attach it to the backing of your quilt.
11. Using the ribbons and referring to "Spider-Web Rose" on page 78, stitch a rose with leaves over the Velcro dot on the left flap.

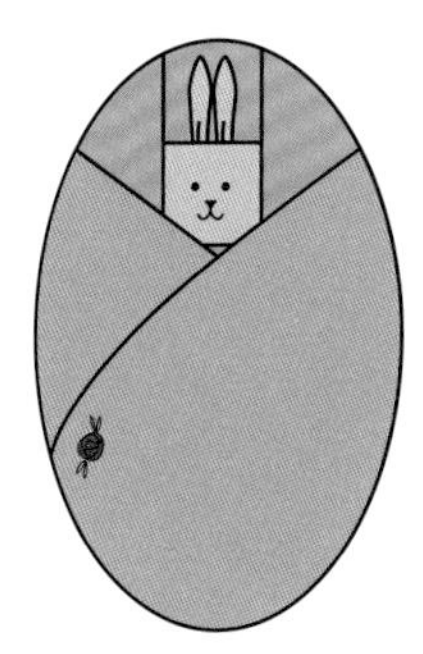

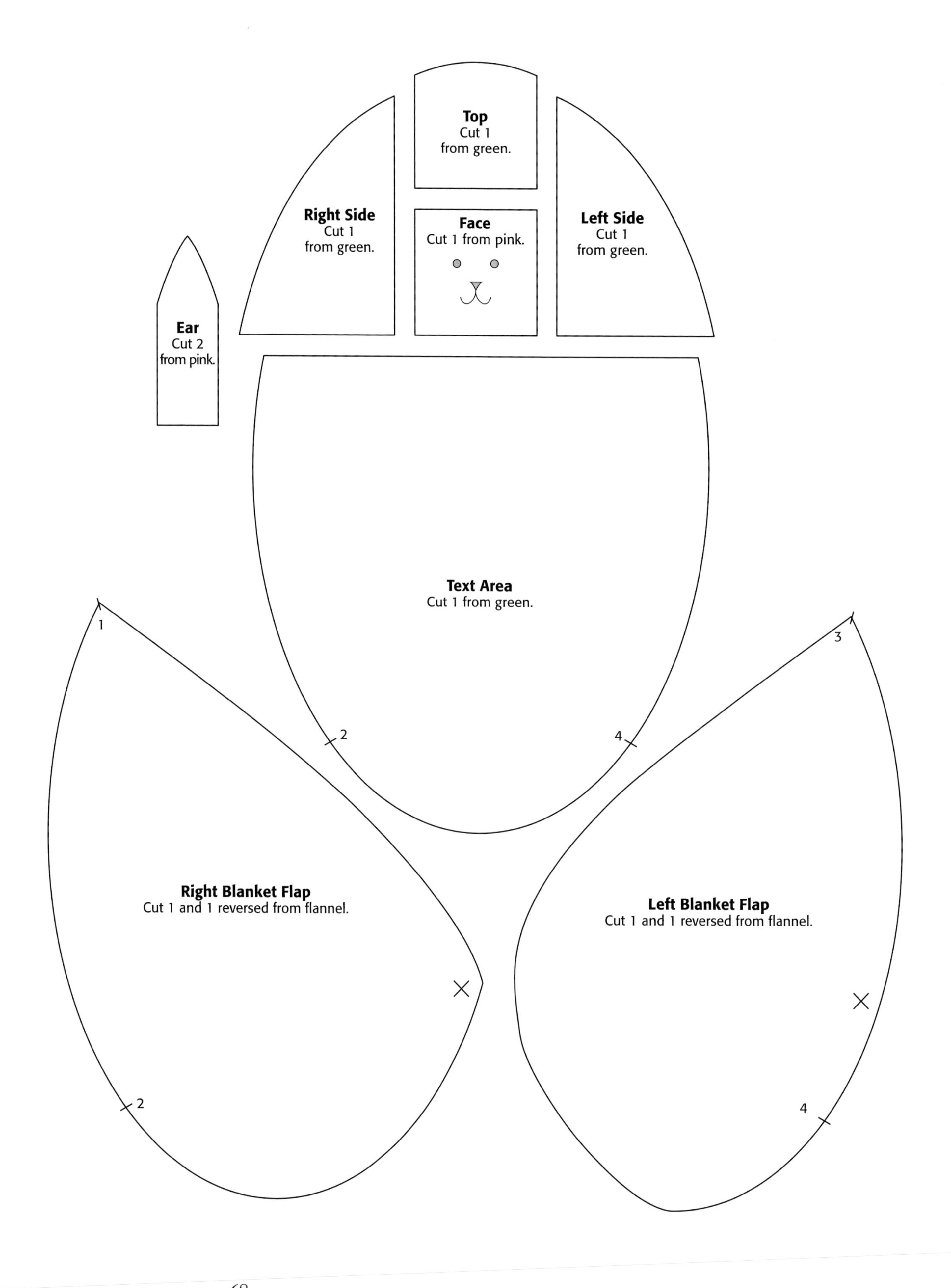
Top
Cut 1
from green.
Right Side
Cut 1
from green.
Face
Cut 1 from pink.
Left Side
Cut 1
from green.
Ear
Cut 2
from pink.
Text Area
Cut 1 from green.
1
2
4
3
Right Blanket Flap
Cut 1 and 1 reversed from flannel.
Left Blanket Flap
Cut 1 and 1 reversed from flannel.
2
4

NIGHT-NIGHT BUNNIES

Put these sleeping bunnies on a quilt or pillow. They'll quickly become part of the bedtime routine for small folks.

Dimensions: 4" x 5"

This label also makes a nice pocket for a tooth fairy pillow.

Materials

- Scraps of quilt backing fabric for background
- Scraps of white imitation suede for bunny faces and ears
- Scrap of turquoise cotton for label
- Freezer paper
- Medium-point permanent marker for tracing onto freezer paper
- Fine-point black permanent marker for making bunny faces

Making the Label

Follow these steps to make a bunny label.

1. Compose your label, formatting the lettering to fit inside a 3½" x 1½" space. If your lettering won't fit in a space of this size, refer to "Enlarging Patterns" on page 18 to resize the project. Letter the turquoise fabric, referring to the lettering instructions on pages 15–23 as needed.
2. Assemble three bunny faces, with ears, from the imitation suede, referring to "Animal Labels" on page 61. Don't mark the faces yet.
3. From the backing fabric, cut one 1½" x 1½" square, two 1" x 1½" rectangles, two 1½" x 2" rectangles, and one 1½" x 4½" rectangle. Sew the bunny faces and flannel pieces into rows as shown. Sew the rows together and press the seam allowances as shown.

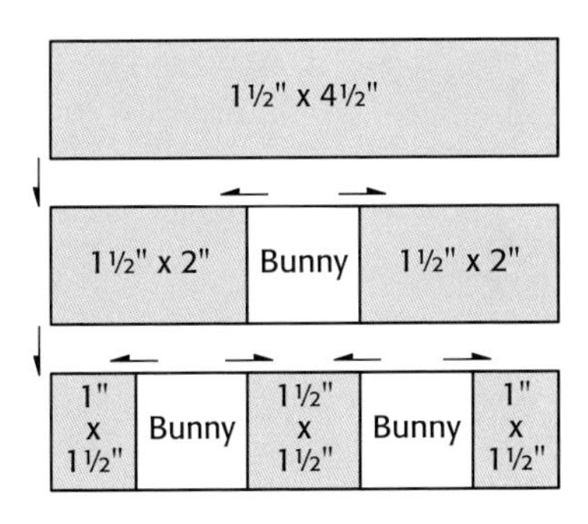

4. Using the medium-point permanent marker, trace the pattern from page 70 onto freezer paper and cut it out on the marked lines. Center the template, shiny side down, over the right side of the lettered fabric. If necessary, you can peel off the freezer paper and reposition it. Cut around the edge of the template. Remove the freezer paper.
5. Sew the lettered label to the bunny unit, pressing the seam allowance toward the label.
6. Draw sleeping bunny faces with the fine-point permanent marker, referring to the placement guide on page 70.
7. Turn under a ¼" seam allowance around the edges of the label and attach it to the backing of your quilt.

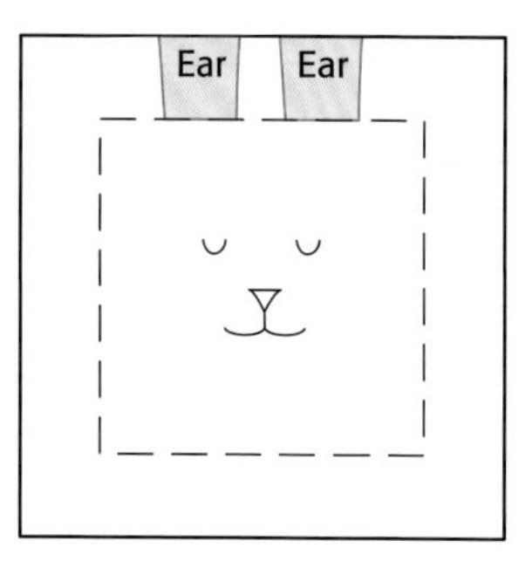

Night-Night Bunnies and Some Bunny Loves You Placement Guide

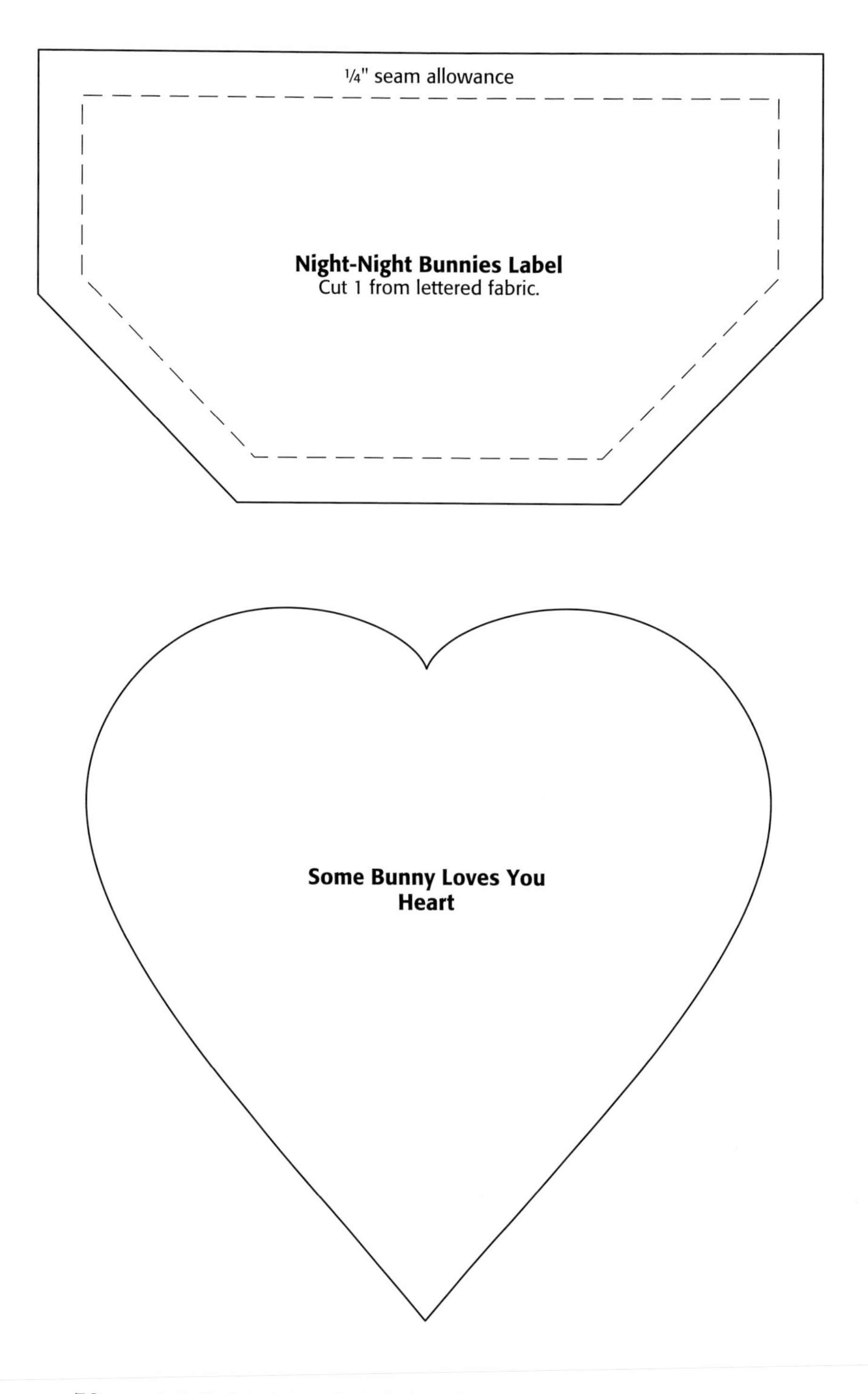

SOME BUNNY LOVES YOU

USE THIS heart-shaped bunny label to convey the love you put into your quilt.

DIMENSIONS: 3½" x 4"
This small label is great for doll quilts. Computer lettering on iron-on transfer film allowed me to fit a lot of information in a small area.

Materials

- Scrap of green fabric for background
- Scraps of fabric for bunny face
- Scraps of imitation suede for bunny ears
- Freezer paper
- Medium-point permanent marker for tracing onto freezer paper
- Fine-point permanent marker for drawing the bunny face

Making the Label

Follow these steps to make a bunny label.

1. Assemble a bunny face, with ears, referring to "Animal Labels" on page 61. Don't mark the face yet.
2. Cut a 3" x 4¼" rectangle of green fabric for the text area. Compose your label, formatting the text to fit a triangular area measuring 2¼" x 2". If your lettering won't fit in an area of this size, refer to "Enlarging Patterns" on page 18 to resize the project. Letter the fabric, referring to the lettering instructions on pages 15–23 as needed.
3. From the green fabric, cut one 1½" x 1½" square for the top of the head and two 2" x 2½" rectangles for the sides of the face. Sew the 1½" square to the top of the bunny's head. Press the seam allowance toward the face to make the ears stand up. Sew a 2" x 2½" green rectangle to each side of the face. Press the seam allowances away from the face.

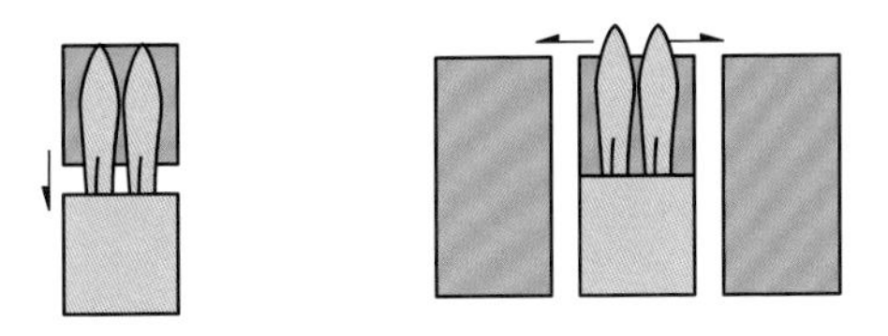

4. Stitch the text rectangle to the bottom of the face unit, centering the text. Press the seam allowance toward the text rectangle.

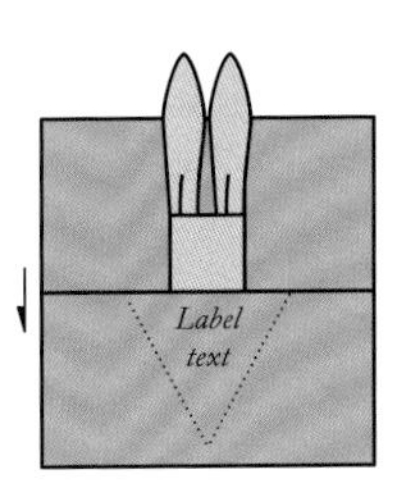

5. Draw the bunny face with the fine-point marker, referring to the placement guide on page 70.
6. Pin the ears out of the way, down over the face. Using the medium-point marker, trace the heart shape from page 70 onto freezer paper and cut it out on the marked lines. Press the template, shiny side down, to the wrong side of the bunny label, checking to make sure that the heart is centered over the text. If necessary, you can peel off the freezer paper and reposition it. Cut out the heart shape, adding a ¼" seam allowance. Turn under the seam allowance and press it in place. Remove the freezer paper and attach the label to the backing of your quilt.

JOEY AND HIS MAMA

A FAVORITE marsupial lives in his mama's pouch. The lettering shown in the photo was composed on a computer, printed onto iron-on transfer film, and then applied to fabric.

DIMENSIONS: 4" x 7¼"
A ribbon tether keeps Joey near Mama.

Materials

If your lettering won't fit a 2¼" x 2½", refer to "Enlarging Patterns" on page 18 to resize the project.

- 7" x 12" piece of tan cotton for front panel and pouch
- 6" x 10" piece of dark brown flannel for Mama
- Two 9" x 9" squares of light brown cotton for Joey
- 9" x 9" square of polyester batting
- 12" length of narrow ribbon for tether
- 3½" length of ¼"-wide elastic
- Small safety pin
- 7" round embroidery hoop
- Freezer paper
- Tan and dark brown cotton thread
- Transparent thread for attaching label to quilt backing (optional)
- Medium-point permanent marker for tracing patterns onto freezer paper
- Fine-point permanent black marker for faces
- Pencil or air-soluble marker

Making Mama

Follow these steps to make the Mama label.

1. Using a permanent marker, trace the pattern pieces for the Mama body, front panel, and pouch from page 74 onto the uncoated side of freezer paper. Include all dots and numbers. Cut out the shapes on the marked lines.
2. Press the shiny side of the templates onto the wrong sides of the tan and dark brown fabrics, and mark around the templates. Using the pencil or air-soluble marker, transfer all marks to the fabric. Cut out the pieces, adding ¼" seam allowances to Mama's body and Mama's front panel. The seam allowances are included in the pouch pattern.
3. Compose your label, formatting it to fit a 2¼" x 2½" area. Letter the text onto the upper half of the front panel, referring to the lettering instructions on pages 15–23 as needed.
4. Make a casing at the top of the pouch by folding under ¼" and then another ¾" (along the dotted lines). Using the tan thread, topstitch ⅝" from the upper edge of the folded fabric. Attach the safety pin to one end of the elastic and secure the other end of the elastic to the seam allowance with a straight pin. Insert the safety-pinned end into the casing and ease the pin all the way through the fabric. Remove the safety pin and secure the elastic. Sew the elastic by stitching across both ends of the casing, ⅛" from the sides.
5. With right sides facing up, pin the pouch to the front panel, matching dots 1 and easing in the fullness at the bottom. Stay stitch ⅛" from the sides and bottom. Turn under the edges and position the front panel, right side up, on the right side of the body piece, matching dots 2 and 3. Topstitch the panel to the body.

6. Using the fine-point permanent marker, add the facial features.
7. Turn under the edges of Mama's body and press. Attach the label to the backing of your quilt, using the transparent thread and referring to "Invisible Machine Appliqué" on page 33.

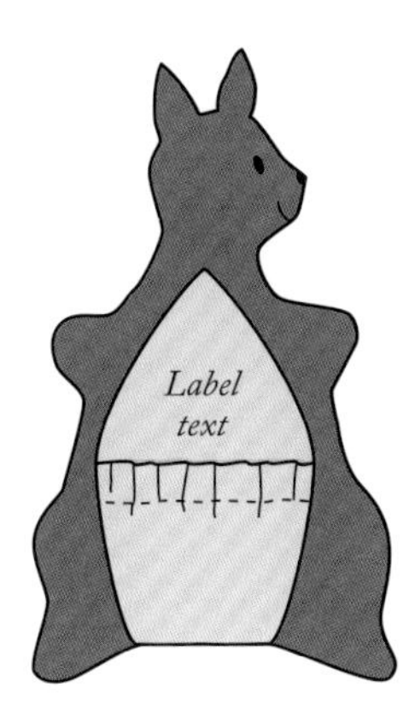

Making Joey

Follow these steps to make Joey.

1. Using the medium-point permanent marker, trace the Joey pattern from page 74 onto the uncoated side of freezer paper and cut it out on the marked lines. Press the shiny side of the template to the right side of a 9" square of light brown fabric.
2. Place the second light brown square right side down; then put the 9" batting square on top. Place the square with the template on top of the batting, with the right side facing up. Place the layered quilt sandwich in the embroidery hoop, with the inner hoop on the same side as the Joey figure.

3. To set your sewing machine for a satin stitch, tighten the bobbin tension slightly and loosen the top tension a little bit. The bobbin thread should not be visible on the right side of the fabric. Select a medium-width zigzag stitch and shorten the stitch length so that your stitches will lie very close together, with no fabric showing through them. Thread the top and bobbin of your machine with dark brown thread. Satin stitch around the Joey figure, just outside the freezer-paper template. Remove the sandwich from the embroidery hoop and then remove the freezer paper. Cut out the Joey figure just outside the stitching.

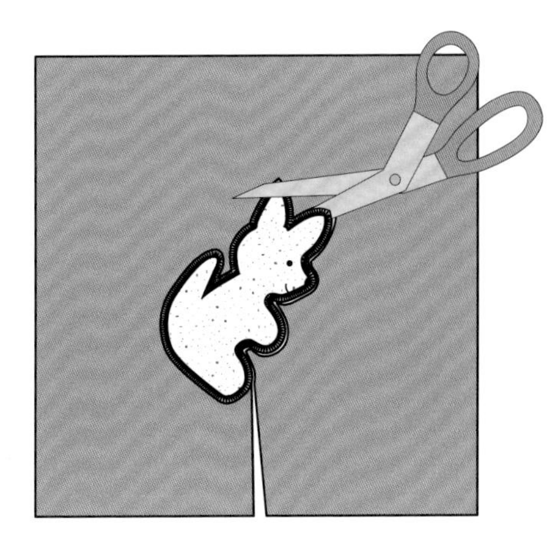

4. Using the fine-point permanent marker, draw features on Joey's face, referring to the pattern on page 74. Sew one end of the 12" ribbon to Joey and the other end inside Mama's pouch. Tuck Joey into the pouch.

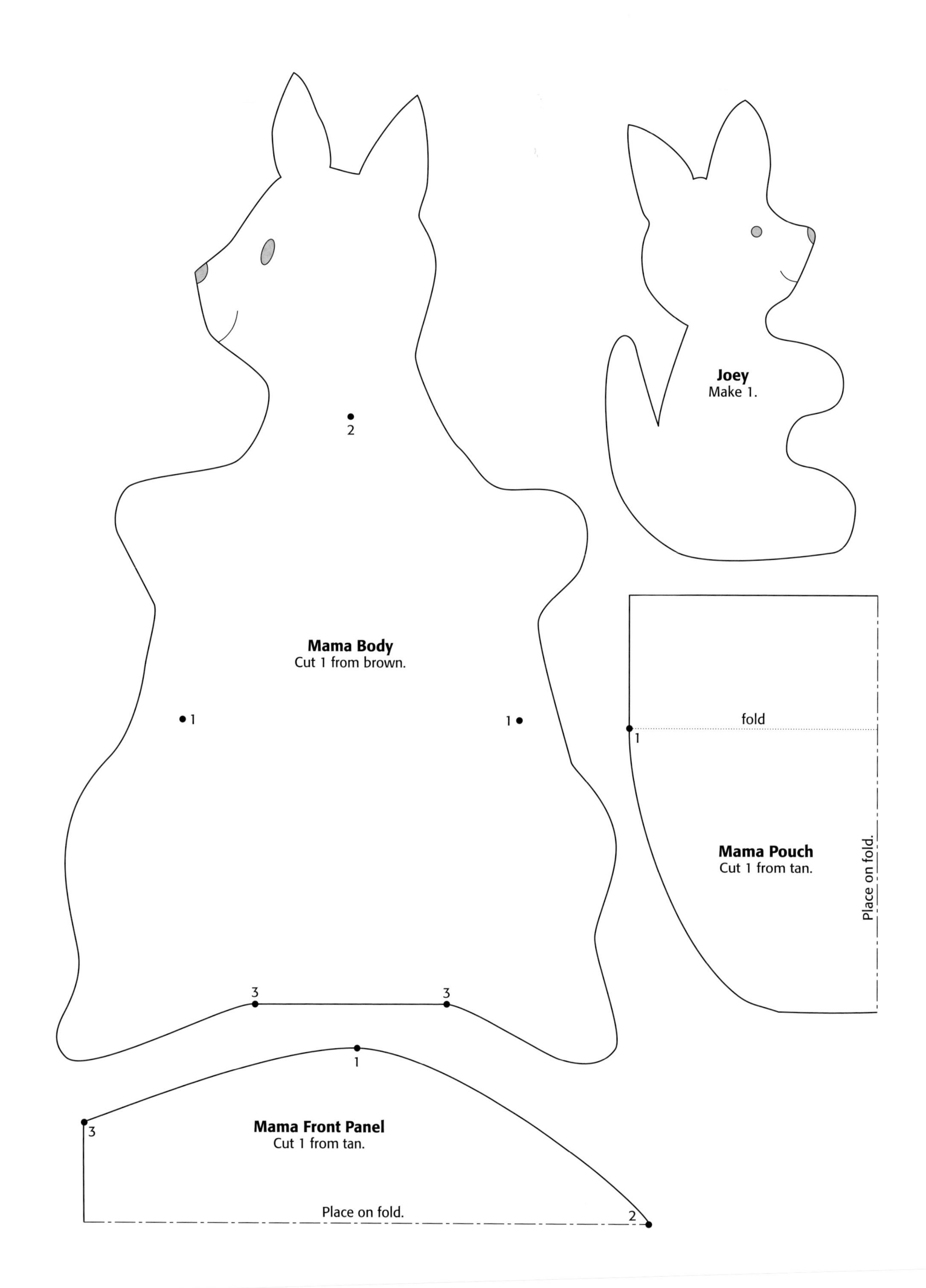
Joey
Make 1.
2
Mama Body
Cut 1 from brown.
1
1
fold
1
Mama Pouch
Cut 1 from tan.
Place on fold.
3
3
1
3
Mama Front Panel
Cut 1 from tan.
Place on fold.
2

Adapting a Child's Drawing

Make a label or soft quilted ornament that will become a family treasure. Start with a child's drawing, simplifying the image if necessary to smooth out edges and curves, and then use it as a pattern for the "Joey" technique on page 73. Shown below are some motifs that I have used.

TEXTURE WHEELS FOR BABIES AND TODDLERS

Children love to feel the soft, smooth, and fuzzy textures on these labels.

Dimensions: 9¼" diameter

One label provides four different textures for a baby to explore.

Materials

- Label, printed on iron-on transfer film (see page 20)*
- 6" x 6" squares of 3 fabrics with different textures (satin, velvet, fleece, or silk)
- 6" x 6" square of light green cotton for lettered triangle
- Compass and pencil or a round object to trace around
- Medium-point black permanent marker
- Freezer paper

*The text should fit into a 2¼" x 3¾" triangle. If your text is too large for an area this size, refer to "Enlarging Patterns" on page 18 to resize the pattern.

Making the Label

Follow these steps to make a texture-wheel label.

1. Referring to the iron-on transfer manufacturer's instructions, apply the lettering to the inner corner of the cotton square, orienting it as shown below.
2. Sew the four squares together as shown to make a Four Patch block.

3. Measure the block from the center of the block to the outer edge of the lettering, and then add ½" to that measurement. Using the permanent marker, draw a circle of that radius onto freezer paper and cut it out on the marked line. Press the shiny side of the circle template to the wrong side of the Four Patch block. Cut out the label ⅜" from the edge of the freezer-paper circle. Make long basting stitches ⅛" from the edge of the circle and pull up the thread to gather the fabric over the edge of the template. Press.

At left, the circle edge is turned over the freezer-paper template. At right, the edge of the label is basted and ready for appliqué.

4. Attach the label to the backing of your quilt, referring to "Invisible Machine Appliqué" on page 33. Cut away the backing fabric behind the label, leaving a ¼" seam allowance beyond the template edge. Remove the freezer paper.

Creative Borders and Accents

You can decorate a quilt label in many ways. Explore the following methods and see if you can come up with ideas of your own.

DECORATIVE MACHINE STITCHING

The decorative stitches on many of today's sewing machines can be used for borders around quilt labels. You can also use decorative machine stitching to secure a label to a quilt. Even a functional stitch, such as a long, straight stitch or a basting stitch, looks nice when made in heavy thread next to a pinked fabric edge.

Dimensions: 8" x 5"
Machine star stitches, echoing the flag print, hold the lettered fabric to the label background.

Dimensions: 5¼" x 4¼"
Machine embroidery frames a hand-inked label.

STENCILING

Use stencils to add borders and decorative motifs to your labels. For labels, I like the miniature brass stencils sold for embossing and stenciling stationery. All sorts of stencils can be found in craft and art-supply stores.

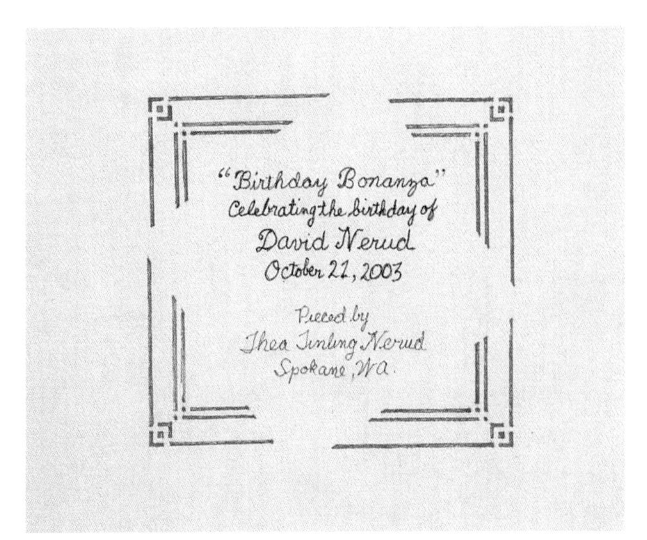

Dimensions: 4½" x 4½"
A stenciled border sets off the lettering in this simple ink-on-fabric label. I used a frame-corner stencil from American Traditional.

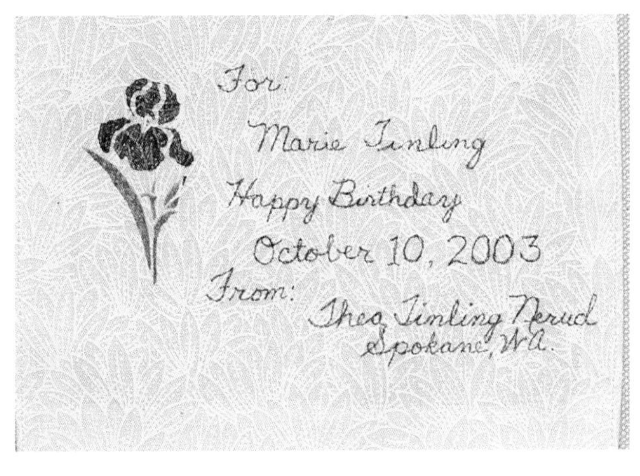

Dimensions: 6" x 5"
I stenciled this American Traditional iris with a purple fabric pen. For the leaves and stems I used green stencil paint.

Materials for Stenciled Label

- Label fabric in color and size of your choice
- Stencil of your choice
- Stencil brush
- Fabric paints in desired colors
- Masking tape
- Paper towels

Stenciling the Fabric

Follow these steps to stencil a label.

1. Tape the label fabric, right side up, to a smooth, hard, paint-resistant surface such as a metal or glass tray. Position the stencil on the fabric and tape it in place. Tape over any portions of the stencil where you don't want to feature the first color of paint.
2. Work the first paint color into the brush, and then tap it on a paper towel until it is almost dry. Apply the paint with the stencil brush around the edges of the stencil openings, using a straight up-and-down tapping motion. Allow the paint to dry thoroughly. Clean the brush after you finish using the first paint color.

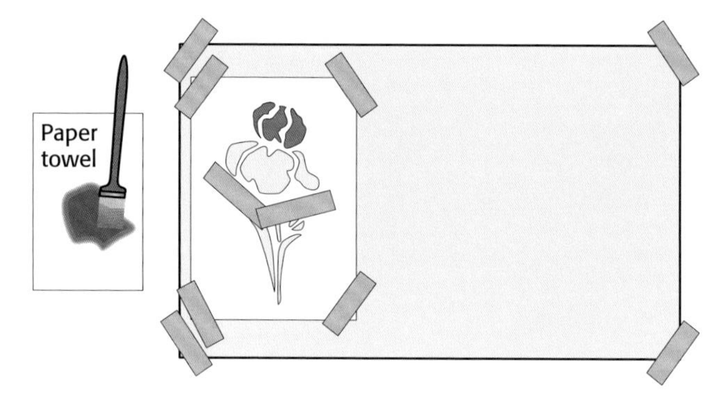

3. Remove the tape from any areas that will receive the second paint color—don't move the stencil itself until you've applied all of the colors. Tape over any areas that won't receive the second color. Apply the second paint color with the stencil brush. Allow the paint to dry thoroughly. Continue in this manner until you have applied all of the paint colors. Carefully remove the stencil to avoid smearing the paint. Allow the paint to dry completely. Some paints need to be heat-set to make them permanent. Follow the paint manufacturer's directions.

Stenciling with Permanent Markers

You can color your fabric with permanent markers instead of paint. Check to be sure that the point of any pen you use is small enough to fit through the stencil openings. Tape the fabric and stencil in place, as above, and proceed to fill each area with the ink color you've chosen.

SPIDER-WEB ROSE

An exquisite spider-web rose adds a delicate touch to a label.

A silk-ribbon rose from the "Baby Bunny Bunting" label shown on page 66.

Materials

- Label fabric
- 12" length of 7 mm pink silk ribbon
- 12" length of 7 mm green silk ribbon
- Pink or white cotton thread for hand sewing
- Size 10 Sharp needle
- Embroidery needle with eye large enough for 7 mm silk ribbon

Making the Rose

Follow these steps to make a spider-web rose.

1. Thread the Sharp needle with two strands of thread. Bring the needle up through the fabric and take five ¼"-long straight stitches, radiating the stitches from a central point.

2. Thread the embroidery needle with the pink ribbon and insert the needle tip through the short end of the ribbon. Slide the ribbon down the needle shank to anchor it in place. Fold over the other end of the ribbon ¼". Insert the needle into the center and pull the ribbon through, making a flat, square ribbon knot.

3. Bring the needle up through the center of the radiating stitches and then weave it under and over the stitches, making sure to keep the ribbon somewhat loose. Allow the ribbon to twist as you work, to create texture in the petals. Continue weaving the ribbon until all five straight stitches have been filled. End by taking the needle to the wrong side of your work near the outer edge of the rose. Secure the ribbon by taking two little stitches underneath the rose. Clip the ribbon ¼" from the surface of the fabric.

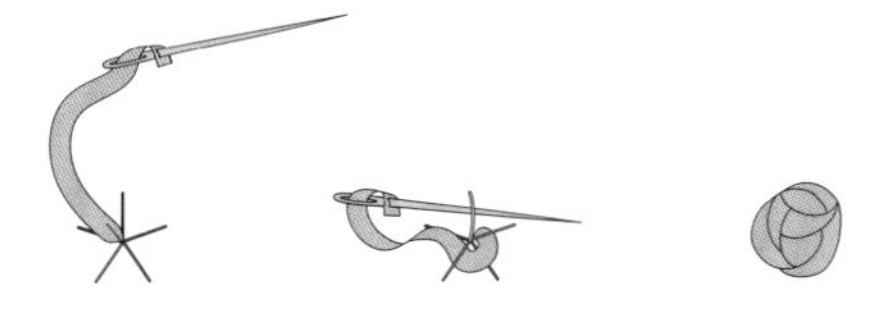

4. Thread the embroidery needle with the green ribbon and insert the needle tip through the short end of the ribbon. Slide the ribbon down the needle shank to anchor it. Bring the needle up near the rose at point A and then insert it approximately ¼" away at point B, as shown. Repeat this straight stitch to make as many leaves as you want. Secure the ribbon to the back of your work by weaving the ribbon under the stitches, and clip the ribbon ¼" from the surface of the fabric.

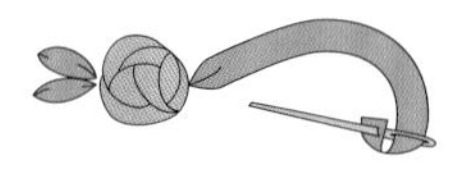

Bibliography

Buck, Karen. *The Crematory Cat,* Lincoln, Nebraska: iUniverse, Inc., 2003.

Hargrave, Harriet. *Mastering Machine Appliqué,* Lafayette, California: C&T Publishing, 1991.

Mathieson, Judy. *Mariner's Compass Quilts: New Directions,* Lafayette, California: C&T Publishing, 1995.

Pappas, Dina. *More Quick Watercolor Quilts,* Woodinville, Washington: Martingale & Company, 2001.

Pappas, Dina. *Quick Watercolor Quilts: The Fuse, Fold, and Stitch Method,* Woodinville, Washington: Martingale & Company, 1999.

Sources

CHECK YOUR LOCAL quilt shop first for fabrics, notions, books, information, and inspiration. If they don't have what you're looking for, they'll probably know where you should look next. To learn more about specific products, you can also contact the following companies.

AMERICAN TRADITIONAL DESIGNS
800-448-6656
www.americantraditional.com
Stencils and stenciling tools

C. JENKINS NECKTIES
314-521-7544 ext. 22
www.cjenkinscompany.com
Bubble Jet Set 2000, Bubble Jet Rinse, Miracle Fabric Sheets printable fabric

HEWLETT-PACKARD DEVELOPMENT COMPANY
www.hp.com/go/quilting
Quilt label software, transfer paper, printable fabric, printer ink, printers, fun quilting Web site

JUNE TAILOR
www.junetailor.com
800-844-5400
Printable fabrics, transfer sheets

MARTINGALE & COMPANY
800-426-3126
www.martingale-pub.com
Photo Transfer Paper

NANCY'S NOTIONS
www.nancysnotions.com
Sensuede imitation suede

OFFICE DEPOT, INC.
www.officedepot.com
800-463-3768
Iron-on transfers, Sanford Sharpie Ultra-Fine Point markers, printer ink, software, and hardware

MILLIKEN AND COMPANY
www.printedtreasures.com
Printed Treasures printable fabric

SAKURA COLOR PRODUCTS OF AMERICA
www.gellyroll.com
Pigma Micron pens

About the Author

Super Shots Portrait Studio, Spokane, WA

THEA NERUD has loved sewing ever since she can remember. Her grandma taught her to embroider when she was four or five years old, "mainly to keep me out of mischief," Thea says. Her mother encouraged her first sewing efforts, letting Thea try things and make messes, giving her instruction and assistance whenever she asked for it. Making clothing for herself and family members, and down sleeping bags, made up Thea's sewing projects for years. She started making quilts in 1965.

Grandchildren, gardening, pets, and wildlife are Thea's greatest joys. Sewing machines and computers are her favorite toys. Her favorite respite and creative recharge is the Empty Spools Seminar at Asilomar Conference Grounds in Monterey, California, with her cousin from California as a roommate.

Thea retired from nursing in 2002. She now has time to use her new quilt room and has just started teaching quilt-label classes. She lives in Spokane, Washington, where she hand feeds the chickadees and chipmunks, and the bluebirds come when she whistles. To find out what's new with Thea, visit www.theaquilts.com